A.W. To

Compiled and Edited by James L. Snyder

PREPARING
FOR
JESUS'
RETURN

DAILY LIVE THE BLESSED HOPE

Regal

For more information and
special offers from Regal Books, email us at
subscribe@regalbooks.com

Published by Regal
From Gospel Light
Ventura, California, U.S.A.
www.regalbooks.com
Printed in the U.S.A.

Library of Congress Cataloging-in-Publication Data
Tozer, A. W. (Aiden Wilson), 1897-1963.
Preparing for Jesus' return / A.W. Tozer.
p. cm.
Includes bibliographical references and index.
ISBN 978-0-8307-6395-5 (trade paper : alk. paper)
1. Second Advent—Biblical teaching. I. Title.
BT886.3.T69 2012
236'.9—dc23
2012026701

Rights for publishing this book outside the U.S.A. or in non-English languages are
administered by Gospel Light Worldwide, an international not-for-profit ministry.
For additional information, please visit www.glww.org, email info@glww.org, or write
to Gospel Light Worldwide, 1957 Eastman Avenue, Ventura, CA 93003, U.S.A.

To order copies of this book and other Regal products in bulk quantities,
please contact us at 1-800-446-7735.

CONTENTS

LIVING THE BLESSED HOPE

No biblical truth drew closer to the heart of A. W. Tozer than the imminent return of the Lord Jesus Christ. This focus on our Blessed Hope dictated much of his passion to encourage believers to rise above the times and fix their gaze on Jesus, our soon-coming King. He taught that for those who are ready for Jesus' return, there is no calamity raging around them that can shake the quiet assurance and confidence that Jesus Christ *will* return.

Tozer was not known in his day as a Bible prophecy teacher, and yet he did his share of teaching on the subject. He referred to Bible prophecy as "prehistory," and he created this series of messages on the book of Revelation to spur every believer on to get ready and stay ready in this season that leads up to the Lord's return. The Blessed Hope is what Tozer looked for and what he lived for.

Tozer believed that an important reason why prophecy should be pursued today is because of the abuses down the years. Almost every generation has had its share of "the End is Near" people claiming to know the time and day of our Lord's return, despite the clear teaching in the Bible that "of that day and hour knoweth no man" (Matt. 24:36).

Some headline-seeking preachers, it seems to me, hope that Christ will give them some leeway or at least enough time so that they can write a book and become known as the one who accurately predicted the return of the Lord. Thankfully, our Lord does not give credence to such absolute nonsense.

Right up front, Tozer points out the difference between the evangelical mystic and the evangelical rationalist when it comes to the book of Revelation. Here is where some will probably find occasion to pause and wonder which side they are going to be on. Tozer explains, "The evangelical mystic, like John, stands in the presence of the awesome God and cries 'holy, holy, holy,' and falls down at His feet as dead. But the evangelical rationalist figures it all out and says, 'We can understand it, we know how it is,' then writes a long book about it, telling exactly what it is like."

As you might well know, Tozer aligned himself with the evangelical mystic. This is how he approached Bible prophecy—not to fit in every little piece and person, but rather to focus on the Lord Jesus Christ as coming again. It is, after all, the revelation, or unveiling, of Jesus Christ.

I think an important emphasis in this book is that no matter what your beliefs are about the timing of the coming of the Lord, you *should not* make your particular view of Bible prophecy the litmus test for believer fellowship. We can disagree without being disagreeable. We can hold different views without disrupting our fellowship. This is the ploy of the enemy—to get God's people to fight about their particular slice of Bible prophecy and not realize it as part of the whole pie.

Instead of Bible prophecy being the great divider, it should unite us all around our risen and glorified Lord who will soon appear. No matter which angle you are looking from, the center of your focus is Jesus Christ. So let us not argue over the right sleeve of Christ's robe in contrast to the left sleeve. We need both sleeves to make a robe, and we need the whole of Bible prophecy to bring the focus onto the person of the Lord Jesus Christ.

Tozer's message does not offer speculation, but hope. In the midst of our times, we need to look up, for our "redemption draweth nigh" (Luke 21:28). We are almost out of time, but in the meantime, we are to occupy until He comes. We are not to be occupied with trying to figure out the exact day or time. Rather, we are to daily live with the knowledge that He could come at any moment, while at the same time we continue to accomplish the work He has given us to do.

When Tozer started his ministry, he was a fiery evangelist. He held evangelistic meetings in churches, campgrounds and wherever he could get an audience, which sometimes meant on street corners. As he grew older, his emphasis began to change toward the deeper Christian life. Even though Tozer preached these sermons during the last two or three years of his life, there is still a strong evangelistic element to them. No matter where he starts, no matter what his topic, he always brings a person to bear upon these thoughts: *What will you do with Jesus Christ right now?* and, *Are you ready for His coming?*

The best compliment Tozer could ever receive from this book is that it created within your heart an overwhelming passion for the Lord Jesus Christ, our Blessed Hope.

"Even so, come, Lord Jesus" (Rev. 22:20).

Rev. James L. Snyder

Preparing for Jesus' Return

1

THE SEASON OF THE BLESSED HOPE

Heavenly Father, I bow before You in humble expectation
of Thy grace and goodness. May my heart be prepared in
righteousness and holiness to receive Thee when Thou comest.
I live each day in the expectation of Thy soon return.
May I daily live the Blessed Hope. Amen.

Bible prophecy is a subject that carries a great deal of religious baggage. Eliminating that baggage and getting to the core is the aim of this book. To do that will require two things: *caution* and *courage*. We must cautiously take care not to allow the focus of our study to stray from Jesus Christ; and we must courageously keep the central purpose of the Blessed Hope—our Lord's return—in view so that we don't get stuck in the quagmire of religious trivialities. As I have prepared this teaching, I have prayed for wisdom to know the difference.

The purpose of Bible prophecy is not to alarm us but rather to alert us to the times so that we can prepare for the return of Jesus—one of the great themes in the Bible and one that brings comfort and encouragement to the believer; hence the phrase "the Blessed Hope." In a world filled with all kinds of uncertainty, the believer possesses the comfort of the Blessed Hope, which means Jesus will soon return.

I readily acknowledge that Bible prophecy is a fertile field for religious cults and scams and has been the downfall of much in Christianity today. Heresies associated with Bible prophecy, especially the book of Revelation, have caused many to turn away from the subject altogether. Although heresies abound in this area, I will not deviate from what the Bible teaches, because prophecy is the Blessed Hope of the believer.

After reading many books on prophecy and revelation, I have concluded that some prophecy teachers think they know more about prophecy than the apostle John who wrote the book of Revelation. How they came upon their knowledge is more than I can understand. They know more than Daniel; they are wiser than Isaiah; and they see further into the future than the beloved apostle John. These pseudo-prophetic teachers make predictions that these wise old men of God never would have made. They understood the purpose of Bible prophecy, while many of these modern prophetic teachers do not; consequently, they major in surface incidentals.

I shall not spend my time or yours focusing on the outer shell of Bible prophecy. Rather, I will delve into the deep core of what it is all about. The supreme purpose of prophecy is to alert us to the fact that Jesus is coming. By looking at what the Bible has to say about prophecy, we begin to understand the nature and character of the one who will soon return, even the Lord Jesus Christ.

His Coming Is Sure

During His public ministry, our Lord taught His disciples that He would return to earth again. Consequently, all of the apostles taught that Jesus would return. Down through the years, the church fathers held to this truth that Jesus Christ will come back to earth again. Even the very angels dressed in white that saw Him go off into heaven said, "Ye men of Galilee, why stand ye gazing up into heaven? this same Jesus, which is taken up from you into heaven, shall so come in like manner as ye have seen him go into heaven" (Acts 1:11).

For the serious Bible student, there is no question that Jesus will return. To read the Bible and not come to that conclusion is the epitome of hypocrisy. When I talk about the Second Coming, I realize that a variety of views are tossed about by some of these so-called prophecy experts.

In trying to understand and explain the Second Coming, some have said that it was death. Of course, that would mean that every time a Christian died it was the return of the Lord again to earth. The Scriptures teach that Christ came and will come for two events: the first was to die and the second is to reign. Therefore, if Christ came every time a Christian died, it would mean Christ's return had to be repeated every time a Christian died. This is a misunderstanding of Christ's return.

I am not sure how these "prophecy experts" got to this point of view, but it undermines the whole concept of the Blessed Hope. Our hope is not in the fact that one day we shall die, but that Jesus Christ, in all of His glory, shall return to earth to rule and reign. This is what I am looking for; it is what I live for.

Based upon my understanding of Scripture, I firmly believe that we are living in great days that are grand and dramatic. I refer to this as the season of the Blessed Hope. Not even the ubiquitous news media can possibly have a true concept of how great, grand and solemn the times are in which we are now living. The very atmosphere of our times is conducive to the Blessed Hope. "Look up, and lift up your heads" (Luke 21:28).

Although we know for sure that He is coming, we know not when. There is the twist. We are helpless to predict when He is actually coming back. Since the apostolic days, nobody has been smart enough or educated enough in the Scriptures to know the exact day and time and hour that Jesus will return. Some offer their suggestions, but all have failed, because nobody can know for sure.

The Bible does not give us a prophetic schedule that, similar to a train schedule, gives out the name of every stop, the time it will arrive and when it will leave. Therefore, to rigidly interpret what the Scripture says is to dishonor the integrity of the Scriptures. The Bible is a book of majestic outlook, telling us of the future in great brush strokes much like an artist painting a picture across the sky. The size is so tremendous that you have to stand back to take it all in. The fine details are lost in the grandeur of the Blessed Hope that Jesus is coming. Even though I am not sure of the time schedule, as long as I am on the train, going in the right direction, it does not really matter what the schedule is.

I do not know what tomorrow will be like. Nobody knows, not even the angels; only our Father who art in heaven knows. If we common people feel helpless to predict tomorrow, do not lose heart, because the great leaders of the world are helpless as well.

And the kings of the earth, and the great men, and the rich men, and the chief captains, and the mighty men, and every bondman, and every free man, hid themselves in the dens and in the rocks of the mountains; and said to the mountains and rocks, Fall on us, and hide us from the face of him that sitteth on the throne, and from the wrath of the Lamb: for the great day of his wrath is come; and who shall be able to stand? (Rev. 6:15-17).

These great men of the earth will cry out for the mountains to fall on them to hide them from the wrath of the Lamb. They are great men all right, but their greatness hid from them the marvelous truth of the Blessed Hope. While they were all about being great, they missed the one true great thing—Jesus Christ.

To give any kind of prediction about world events apart from the Scripture is to practice a form of religious insanity that serves only to confuse people who then finally give up and say, "I can't understand prophecy; I guess it's not for me." Any prediction of our Lord's return that relies on education or technology is sure to be wrong and leads only to discouragement, and finally to abandonment of what the Bible has to say about Jesus' return. The Blessed Hope is for the believer, and it brings comfort, assurance and confidence to the heart of the believer in the midst of this world's turmoil. Our focus is not on the calamity around us, but on His glorious coming. Prophecy is not for the critical or curious eye, but for that eye focused on and looking for the Lord Jesus Christ, the Coming One.

Therefore, the point of Bible prophecy is not to alarm us but to alert us to the circumstances leading up to the Lord's return. This alertness is to spur us on to be ready; and the Bible says a lot about how we can be ready for His return.

Signs of the Lord's Return

Our Lord, in Matthew 24, outlined for us the characteristics of the times leading up to His return. While not divulging the days or the times, He has outlined compelling evidence for those who are worthy to receive it and believe it. There are five characteristics of this season leading up to the return of Jesus Christ.

Messianic Delusions

Jesus pointed out, "For many shall come in my name, saying, I am Christ; and shall deceive many. . . . And many false prophets shall rise, and deceive many" (Matt. 24:5,11). Further on, He explained, "For there shall arise false Christs, and false prophets, and shall shew great signs and wonders; insomuch that, if it were possible, they shall deceive the very elect" (v. 24).

Since the time when Cain killed Abel, there has never been a time when some wild-eyed fanatic did not think he was God or attempt to be the Messiah and redeem the world. This messianic delusion has always been on the earth. But Jesus taught that there would be a season prior to His coming when there would be a high peak season for such delusions. I cannot help but believe that we are seeing some of that right now.

Every generation has had somebody saying, in effect, "I am the Messiah, and I know how to bring peace to the world; and I can lead everybody into the Promised Land." Some of these people have been political, but a great many have been religious. It seems to me that politics and religion have quite a few things in common, particularly when it comes to controlling people and their destiny. The fact of the existence of false Christs is proof of the near coming of Jesus. The counterfeit always argues the real thing. If there is not something real, it could not be counterfeited. The fact that there are a growing number who are claiming to be Christ today is proof that we are coming near to the return of Jesus. And each year seems to get more intense.

Military Prominence

Jesus also indicated that in the last days we should hear of wars and rumors of wars. "See that ye be not troubled," He warned, "for all these things must come to pass, but the end is not yet. For nation shall rise against nation, and kingdom against kingdom: and there shall be famines, and pestilences, and earth-quakes, in divers places" (Matt. 24:6-7). In our generation, we are seeing an increase of military power like never before.

Right after the First World War, there broke out in our country antiwar movements and the rise of the pacifist. Many preachers were pacifists then and declared, "We outlaw war." They even produced manifestos, and according to them, there could be no more war. War was outdated. All of their arguments pointed to the fact that "war will be no more."

A person only has to read history and discover that there has not been a five-minute period from that day to this when there has been peace in the world. The military has taken over little by little. In our country, we had to have an Army but did not care much for it. Basically, we were civilian, and the people ruled. Slowly, this shifted, and more and more we are hearing the military speech of generals and great men telling us which way we are to take and what we need to do. "Wars and rumours of wars. . . . nation shall raise against nation, and kingdom against kingdom" (Matt. 24:6-7).

Try listening to the current news media that does not, in some way, focus on some war around the world. This increase of military activity, Jesus said, was one of the evidences of His soon return.

Malicious Domination

Another characteristic of the season of the Blessed Hope is that many shall betray one another to the point of actually hating one another. It is a proven fact that totalitarian control has been a technique controlling whole nations, and we witnessed that in Russia and China under the Communist rule.

The whole purpose of that depended on subverting the in-dividual so that he did not think in terms of his family or his church, but in terms of world conquest, so that he would sell out his aged mother to get in good with those in charge. It has always been men betraying men: Cain slew Abel in an awful act of anger; Judas betrayed Christ; and men have betrayed each other down through the years. But I believe this is the betrayal season, and the philosophy of betrayal is everywhere throughout the whole world.

Martyrdom of Believers

Jesus said, "Then shall they deliver you up to be afflicted, and shall kill you: and ye shall be hated of all nations for my name's sake" (Matt. 24:9). I need not remind anyone of the persecutions throughout the world, since the day when Hitler rose and turned his hatred against the Jews down to this present hour. The news media tells us what is happening all around the world and how Christians are suffering and even martyred. Persecution is one technique of totalitarianism both in the church and in the state. The closer we get to the return of Jesus, the more persecution will increase and focus on believers around the world.

Moral Decline in the Church

Nobody would question the fact that our city streets are unsafe, and no matter where you go, there is always some threat of violence. The times are getting increasingly wicked, and we now live in the generation of locked doors. When I was a youngster, there was no such thing as locking our doors. Today there is no such thing as an unlocked door.

The iniquity I am referring to here is more than just the world; it has everything to do with the Church. In this generation, we are facing a backslidden Church. I am talking about individuals in the Church, and I want to press two very important questions.

The first question is, How would you describe your passion for the person of Christ? The Scriptures teach that one of the evidences of the last days is this: "And because iniquity shall abound, the love of many shall wax cold" (Matt. 24:12). So, how ardent is your love for the Lord Jesus Christ?

The second question is simply, What has your Christianity cost you? We have become a bunch of well-groomed showpiece Christians behind glass. Our Christianity has cost us nothing. David, that mighty man of God, said, "Neither will I offer burnt offerings unto the LORD my God of that which doth cost me nothing" (2 Sam. 24:24).

Since last week, what has your Christian faith cost you? The man of God says, "Not forsaking the assembling of ourselves together, as the manner of some is; but exhorting one another: and so much the more, as ye see the day approaching" (Heb. 10:25). Many, I am sad to say, are forsaking the assembly of believers.

We come to church when it is convenient. We serve the Lord at our convenience. The center of our entire life is "convenience." This was not so with the Early Church fathers or with the martyrs down through the years, or with the great Reformers and revivalists. Their Christianity cost them dearly. We who are benefiting from the high cost they paid do not appreciate the cost and have trampled underfoot the preciousness of their sacrifice.

What has our faith cost us? Are we offering to God a bloodless sacrifice like Cain, who offered to God that which cost him not one ounce of blood or sweat or tears? Evangelical American Christians allow missionaries to do all the suffering today. We let them leave their homes and go into the jungles and pagan cities around the world. We let them stay away years at a stretch and sleep in thatched roof huts in dangerous neighborhoods.

On the other hand, we who stay behind have big bank accounts, drive expensive cars and somehow believe that thus were the prophets that came before us. What we need to do is fall on our knees and search our hearts; I believe we will be shocked at what we find. As for me, I want my Christianity to cost me something right down to the last gasp. I do not want an easy road or a convenient ministry or something that costs me nothing.

I want to sing along with A. B. Simpson (1843–1919), who wrote a wonderful missionary hymn called "The Regions Beyond":

> To the hardest the places He calls me to go,
> Not thinking of comfort or ease;
> The world may pronounce me a dreamer, a fool,
> Enough if the Master I please.

Signs abound that the evangelical Church, especially in America, is falling away. Today's evangelical Church is being inundated with activities galore. Not even the apostle Paul had as many irons in the fire as many Christians do today. I believe we ought to be working right up to the very end; but many of our activities are simply done for activity's sake. Our activities are not tied in to the Blessed Hope, and they in no way prepare us for the return of Jesus Christ. Our activities are to please ourselves and court the acceptance of the world.

We also need to watch out for the modern moral code. This has infiltrated the Church in this generation as never before. I see a frightening similarity between the world and the Church today along the lines of morality. The average Christian today accepts the world's standard to live by. Yet, our standard is the Bible, and only the Bible prepares us and enables us to live daily in light of the Blessed Hope.

We must get on our knees before our open Bible and allow the Holy Spirit to break our hearts and create a passion for Christ as we've never had before. We must ask for a passion of such a nature that the things of this world will begin to diminish in their attraction for us. A passion for Christ will enable us to rise above our culture and look unto Jesus, the author and finisher of our faith.

Let us be alert to the season in which we are living. It is the season of the Blessed Hope, calling for us to cut our ties with the world and build ourselves on this One who will soon appear. He is our hope—a Blessed Hope enabling us to rise above our times and fix our gaze upon Him.

As Bible-believing Christians, it is imperative that we stay fully alert to the times in which we live. Our enemy is a master deceiver and a con artist of the highest order, diverting our attention from the Blessed Hope with the problems we face every day. Understanding Bible prophecy will create a passion for holy living. To know the Blessed Hope is to live in full expectation of Christ's imminent return. All signs today point to this being the season of the Blessed Hope. Even so, come, Lord Jesus.

Come Then, Lord Jesus
Horatius Bonar (1808–1889)

The church has waited long
Her absent Lord to see;
And still in loneliness she waits,
A friendless stranger she.

How long, O Lord our God,
Holy and true and good,

Wilt thou not judge thy suffering church
Her sighs and tears and blood?

We long to hear thy voice,
To see thee face to face,
To share thy crown and glory then
As now we share thy grace.

Come, Lord, and wipe away
The curse, the sin, the stain,
And make this blighted world of ours
Thine own fair world again.

2

THE BLESSED HOPE AND THE CURSE OF CURIOSITY

Oh God, I come to Thee with a heart impassioned for Thee,
that I may know Thy fullness and purity and not become engrossed
with mere curiosity or trivial aspects of Thy Son's return.
Allow nothing but Thee to fascinate me. Amen.

Although many people approach prophecy and the book of Revelation with a great deal of curiosity, it is absolutely not a subject for the inquisitive. Rather, the Blessed Hope is a powerful enticement for believers to seek to become holy, to be perfect even as He is perfect and to be watchful, waiting for Jesus' return. *When* He returns is not as important as the fact that *we are ready* for Him when He does return. The crucial question is, When He returns, will He find us waiting?

We are to live as though Christ were coming today, but work as though He were not coming for 1,000 years. We are to be ready for Him today, but we are planning, working and praying as though His return is years down the road. In my ministry and the writing of my books, I keep that reality in full view. I am living my life with expectation; I am eagerly waiting and looking to that hour. If I cannot figure out all the details, I will do the best I can to be prepared whenever it happens. I do not want to be like the many whose curiosity about the details of His coming overshadow the fact that He is coming. I refuse to fall into that category.

Three Interpretations of Eschatology

In that regard, I will not be able to confirm anyone's school of eschatology—the study of future things. It seems that whenever somebody begins talking about prophecy and the return of Jesus, people want to know about your school of eschatology. I will have to disappoint my readers about that. To simplify the issue, let me point out that Bible prophecy falls under three main schools of interpretation, particularly when it comes to the book of Revelation.

Preterist School of Interpretation

One of the first interpretations is what is referred to as the preterist view. This simply says that all of the book of Revelation is past and has been fulfilled. Everything has already taken place and what we read is simply a colorful, dramatic history of certain events that happened before John ever wrote the book of Revelation. It has no bearing upon today's life.

Historical School of Interpretation

Then there is the *historical* view, which says that the book of Revelation was in the process of fulfillment, and some of it began to be fulfilled when it was written. It has been in the slow process of fulfillment ever since. The book of Revelation is simply an historical account.

Futurist School of Interpretation

Then there is the *futurist* view, which simply says that everything in the book of Revelation is still awaiting fulfillment. Apart from the first chapter of the book (some say the third chapter), the rest of Revelation remains to be fulfilled. Everything lies in the future. I am quite sure there are other versions based on these three views, and maybe some versions I have not heard about yet. Everyone seems to have closed in on one particular interpretation and shut out everything else.

A Warning in Interpreting Biblical Prophecy

The area of interpretation is where I believe we need to be quite careful. Bogus interpretation and careless prophecy have armed Satan with weapons he uses to bring confusion to the Body of Christ. Whenever prophecy teachers set up a rigid schedule of Bible prophecy and then the events do not unfold as predicted and when predicted, people are disappointed and spiritually let down. Then our enemy takes advantage of the situation to undermine our Blessed Hope. Instead, we should be jealous of the Blessed Hope and never let it get into the hands of the enemy.

There is one warning that I believe I need to make in this area of biblical prophecy. It is simply this: Do not make your view of prophecy or interpretation of prophecy the test of orthodoxy for orthodoxy's sake. Regardless of what we do believe, we need to be careful about making it the litmus test for fellowship. Where the Bible is clear, we need to be clear and dogmatic. Where the Bible is not as clear, we need to be careful that we are not adding or taking away from the Scriptures. The Bible is not to divide us but enable us to focus on Jesus Christ, the Man of Prophecy.

One of the great hymns of the church is "Onward, Christian Soldiers," by Sabine Baring-Gould (1834–1924). It sets down the delightful biblical principle that is much overlooked today. Here is the second stanza:

> Like a mighty Army moves the Church of God;
> Brothers, we are treading where the Saints have trod;
> We are not divided, all one body we,
> One in hope and doctrine, one in charity.

The Blessed Hope is not to divide the Body of Christ. Instead, we are to rally around the person of Jesus Christ, who is soon to come. This needs to be the motivating factor behind our pursuit of Bible prophecy.

We are not to build the First Church of the Futurist, or the First Church of the Preterist, or the First Church of the Historicalites. Throughout Church history, Christians have become quite adept at building theological fences around themselves to keep away others of some different theological viewpoint. The true Church rises above all of these artificial divisions and focuses on looking for the return of Jesus. We can love each other, serve God together, send the gospel to the ends of the earth, pray and sing together and love each other, even if we do not have the same exact views about the return of Jesus.

I quickly acknowledge that I do not know or understand all the details concerning the coming of the Lord Jesus Christ. If you have a different view from mine, I want you to love me, and I am going to love you. The focus of our fellowship is not on the details of Christ's coming, but on the person of the Blessed Hope—"this same Jesus" (Acts 1:11).

The Curse of Curiosity

Recently, I have noticed that the doctrine of the return of Christ—what I have been calling the Blessed Hope—has gone into some decline, amounting almost to a total eclipse, with scarcely anybody preaching about it anymore. Perhaps some feel it is too controversial. I happen to believe that it is at the core of Christianity.

In light of this, I want to point out the evil of a merely curious interest in Jesus' return. I am referring to it as the curse of curiosity. This is, as the book of Revelation says, "the revelation of Jesus Christ." For us to have just some idle curiosity about this and that throughout the book is to be guilty of as near sacrilege as Phineas and Hophni (see 1 Sam. 2:12) when they compromised the sacred aspect of the Ark of the Covenant and took it into battle as a mere relic to stir the emotions of the Israeli soldiers and win the day.

The Blessed Hope is not a gimmick to stir up the emotions so that some preacher can take up an offering. Rather, the Blessed Hope is of such a nature that it stirs up a passion for the person of the Blessed Hope, even the Lord Jesus Christ. It stirs up within us a desire to know Him, even as He is known, and live in expectation of His return. "Even so, come, Lord Jesus" (Rev. 22:20).

Yet many people only want to find some key, identify some symbol, or interpret some person or activity in prophecy. They want to be the first to do so and then write a book about it, and sell it to the public and build a ministry on it. They want a reputation of being an expert on Bible prophecy. Watch out for the expert. These things are beneath the one who sorely desires to know and experience the unveiling of this Man of the book of Revelation.

For a moment, think with me along this line. Suppose we could figure out the whole picture here in Revelation. Suppose we could identify every person. Suppose we could put together all of the pieces and put the timeline in proper order. If such a thing were possible, I want to pose to you a line of questioning.

If we could do that, would we be any dearer to God? How would this affect our relationship to God and our understanding of Him and His grace and His love toward us? If it were true that we would be dearer to God if we could figure out every prophecy, then only those who can put it all together could really be the recipients of God's amazing grace and love. Who, then, could qualify?

Also, would we be any holier? If we could put everything together and identify everybody, what does it contribute to accentuating our holiness before the world around us? Holiness, as taught in the Scriptures, is not based upon knowledge on our part. Rather, it is based upon the resurrected Christ indwelling us and changing us into His likeness. Holiness has nothing to do with what we know and understand, but it has everything to do with the person of Christ and our relationship with Him. "That I might know him," was the impassioned prayer of the apostle Paul (Phil. 3:10).

In the same vein, if we could do all of this, would we be any freer from the bondage of the world? If we knew all of these things perfectly and could put them all together succinctly, would it be of such significance to our daily life that we would be free from the tyranny of worldliness?

What about heaven? If we were to have perfect knowledge of all prophetic things, would it grant us a greater assurance of going to heaven? Would it draw heaven nearer to us? And what about hell? Being an expert in prophecy does not qualify a person for heaven, nor does it disqualify him for hell. The apostle Paul makes it perfectly clear in 1 Corinthians 13:1-2: "Though I speak with the tongues of men and of angels, and have not charity, I am become as sounding brass, or a tinkling cymbal. And though I have the gift of prophecy, and understand all mysteries, and all knowledge; and though I have all faith, so that I could remove mountains, and have not charity, I am nothing."

All of the things mentioned are exterior and only serve to feed the inquisitive appetite of the immature Christian. Those who are merely curious do not intend to allow the truth of the Blessed Hope to impact their life so that they are no longer the same as they were before. They are quite content in who and what they are. To simply be curious is to miss the whole significance of a book like Revelation. It focuses on the superficial and overlooks the deep significance of the truth of the Blessed Hope.

Which Is More Important?

Allow me to take it one step further. Which is more important? The woman clothed with the sun in Revelation 12:1, or the passage in Revelation 12:17 that says, "Keep the commandments of God, and have the testimony of Jesus Christ"? Both the woman and the commandment are in the same chapter, and I think it is infinitely more important that we keep the commandments of Christ and the testimony of Jesus Christ than to know who this woman is.

A great controversy stews over who this woman is. Some say it is the Church. The child mentioned refers to a small prepared group, which some say are the Christians. Some believe this is a picture of Israel, and the child is none other than Christ. Who is she, and who has the right interpretation? Is that important, or is verse 17 more important? "And the dragon was wroth with the woman, and went to make war with the remnant of her seed, which keep the commandments of God, and have the testimony of Jesus Christ" (Rev. 12:17). This verse is often overlooked in this chapter because of the curious speculation about the woman.

What about the 144,000 in Revelation 14:1? Who are they? That is another interesting passage. It amazes me how many people say they are the 144,000. It is rather amusing that every new cult that comes along says that they are the 144,000, and if you joined them, you will be part of the 144,000. Which is more important? To identify this number, or to bring our lives into line with Revelation 14:12? "Here is the patience of the saints: here are they that keep the commandments of God, and the faith of Jesus."

Here is a simple illustration to show what I mean here. Suppose a man is going to go away, and he says to his son, "Johnny, I'm going away, and I'll come back at a certain time. I won't tell you the day when I am coming back. Here is what I want you to do. I want you to obey your mother and keep your room cleaned, and wash behind your ears; and I don't want you to ride your bicycle out on the busy highway." He lays down some rules and regulations for his young son to keep while he is away. Then he says, "If you keep all of these instructions, when I come back, I will have a surprise for you." He names something the boy has been wanting for a long time.

Young Johnny's eyes are bright as he waits for his father to come back. Then he remembers that there is responsibility attached to this and some things he has to do. Every day he looks for his father to return, and he speculates on when and what time and what day. But all to no avail.

Why do you suppose he is anxious for his father to return? Do you think he would like to know the exact day so that the night before he can cram at the last minute to get ready to meet his father? No, I do not think so.

The day comes when his father returns. They have a wonderful reunion, and then the father says, "Johnny, how did you do while I was away?"

"Oh, Dad, I did everything you told me to do."

The father checks with mother to see if everything is all right, and she says, "Yes, it's all right, Daddy. He did exactly what you told him to do. He was perfect."

Then the father says to the son, "Johnny, because you did what I told you to do and kept my commandments, here's the gift I promised you." He unwraps this fabulous thing the boy has been dreaming of for years.

That is exactly where you and I stand regarding the coming of our Lord Jesus Christ. Before He went away, He said, "I'll be back." When He went up from the Mount of Olives, the angel said, "This same Jesus . . . shall so come in like manner as ye have seen him go to heaven" (Acts 1:11). "This same Jesus . . . in like manner," not somebody else in some other manner, but "this same Jesus . . . in like manner as ye have seen him go into heaven." This is the focus of our anticipation.

Jesus said, "Be ye therefore ready also: for the Son of man cometh at an hour ye think not" (Luke 12:40). The reason we are told that He is coming back and given a prognosis of the coming events is not to stimulate idle curiosity, but so that we might be prepared and ready for Him when He comes.

Is it more important to exploit the curiosity element of prophecy in order to get a crowd, or to bear down on the warnings that Bible prophecy brings to our heart? How the novel, the strange and the supernatural arouse our interest! We put so much emphasis on this, thinking that it will do the work of God—that it will do what the Holy Spirit alone can do in our hearts. *If only people could see something spectacular,* we think, *they would come to Christ.* Many build their ministry on this philosophy. Our Lord understood this and said, "If they hear not Moses and the prophets, neither will they be persuaded, though one rose from the dead" (Luke 16:31).

The purpose of Bible prophecy is that we might be prepared for the hour when we shall escape all of these snares and traps and stand before Jesus Christ our Lord, forgiven. After all of this, where is the penitence? Where is the confessing? Where is the cleansing? It has never been "when" He is coming that has stirred the hearts of the saints down through the centuries; it has always been, "this same Jesus" is coming back.

In the very last chapter of the book of Revelation, we read, "Behold, I come quickly: blessed is he that keepeth the sayings of the prophecy of this book" (Rev. 22:7).

Come, Lord, and Tarry Not
Horatius Bonar (1808–1889)

Come, Lord, and tarry not;
Bring the long-looked-for day;
Oh, why these years of waiting here,
These ages of delay?

Come, for thy saints still wait;
Daily ascends their sigh;
The Spirit and the Bride say, Come!
Dost thou not hear the cry?

Come, and make all things new;
Build up this ruined earth,
Restore our faded Paradise,
Creation's second birth.

Come, and begin thy reign
Of everlasting peace;
Come, take the kingdom to thyself,
Great King of righteousness.

3

THE BLESSED HOPE CLEARLY DEFINES CHRISTIANITY

God, our Father, I look humbly to Thee for grace to live life
worthy of Thee. May my life today be lived in such a way as to
anticipate the return of Thy Son, even the Lord Jesus Christ.
May I live this day in the authority of Jesus Christ. Amen.

Christianity is not what somebody said it was in Rome or Constantinople or London or New York. Christianity is what the Holy Spirit said it is in His book.

Christianity is what the prophets, seers, sages, apostles and holy men, who spoke as the Holy Spirit moved them, said it was. This is what we accept when we become Christians. The essence of Christianity is wrapped up in the expectation of Jesus' imminent return, and these five verses in Revelation 1:4-8 constitute a sweeping and comprehensive view of what it is all about. This is what the prophets and the apostles taught; and it accords with all that the New Testament teaches. Right here we have the beating heart of our holy faith and where our Christian interest and future hope lie. The Blessed Hope clearly defines for us what Christianity is all about.

It would be hard to find anywhere in the Scriptures a more concentrated treatment of Christianity than in this first chapter of the book of Revelation. It behooves us to look at these verses rather closely and see what the Holy Spirit is saying. John the Revelator talks about God the Father—who is, who was, and who is to come. He also refers to the sevenfold Holy Spirit who proceeds from the Father. He talks of Jesus Christ, who He is, the Son of the Father, and what He is: Prophet, Priest and King. He talks of what He has done for us—washed us in His precious blood and made us clean and pure before the Father. He has made us kings and priests unto God.

In Revelation 1, Christ makes a mighty declaration that sounds down the centuries to the churches. Through John the apostle, who calls himself "Your brother and companion in tribulation" (Rev. 1:9), the glorified Head of the Church declares, "Grace be unto you, and peace" (v. 4).

Christ has something to say to His Church. This declaration is all-inclusive, but only to those who qualify. They are the servants of Christ who were washed in His blood, who hear, heed and keep His Word. Regardless of the minor differences among believers down through the generations, Christ is speaking to His Church. What He says to His Church does not apply to anybody else, and it certainly cannot apply to the world.

This all-inclusive benediction is also an all-exclusive one. It excludes those who fail to qualify according to Christ's design. It would be my deepest wish, my heart's desire, that this benediction could include the world's population and everybody born of woman; but Scripture and reason forbid me to hold on to this hope. Not everything good that God says about people in the Bible is for everybody, but for His true servants, who must receive this. All things may be objectively true but are not subjectively true. Faith and obedience are necessary to work this transformation.

The tendency is to try to stretch the sayings of the Lord to cover everybody so that His sayings become an umbrella for the entire human race. The simple fact is, these words of His benediction apply only to those who are within the fold, and exclude everybody else. Each of us must decide whether we come under this benediction or are excluded from it.

And so, Christ, the Head of the Church, has something to say to His Church. Because of who He is, it becomes exceedingly important to hear and heed what He is saying to the churches. "He that hath ears let him hear."

The Authority of the Father

There is only one authority, and that is the eternal Father who is and who was and who is to come. One thing we need to understand is that there are no tenses in God Almighty, maker of heaven and earth. Tenses belong to you and me. When we say that God was, is, and is to come, we are not referring to the fact that there are tenses in God, as though God moves from one period of time into another. It would be to think God down to the level of creatures, which we can never do. It is not God's "was." It is yours and mine. When it says "He that was," it does not mean He that was once, but it means that you and I have a "was." We have a past; and because we have a past, God is in that past. And we have a present, and God is in that present. But it is our "was" and our "is."

God Almighty dwells in an eternal now that is unaffected by the passing of time. The sun that rises in the east in the morning does not make God a day older when it sets in the west at night. It does not affect the infinite perfection of this eternal

God. God is sovereign over yesterday, today and forever, which are mere elements of time.

The Authority of the Holy Spirit

If we were to place less emphasis upon scholastic education and more upon the illumination of the Holy Spirit, we would be a wiser, holier, more powerful Church than we are now.

This is the way it works. Most churches start with a few people groaning in the spirit—yearning and longing in the Holy Ghost to have a revival. Revival comes and the church breaks out, spreads its beautiful wings and, in the Spirit, flies away. A generation goes by, and the old saints who prayed the church into existence die and sleep with the fathers, awaiting the resurrection from the dead. Then another generation that knew not Joseph rises and looks around for power, and they do not have it because they have not paid the price their fathers paid. So they say, "There's only one thing to do: establish schools and get some education. We're going to have some intellectual acumen to meet the challenge of the world." So they build themselves schools, colleges, seminaries and universities. And for the first generation, they are Christian. That, however, is not the end of the story.

The second generation is what I will call quasi-Christian. The third-generation goes to the dogs, theologically, and becomes liberal; and that is the church God turns from and starts another one.

That is the way the Church has come down the years. What we need today is an endowment of the Holy Spirit and the Spirit of wisdom and understanding and counsel and might and knowledge and fear (see Isa. 11:2). When we have this endowment of the Holy Ghost, and His sevenfold perfection, we will have less need for other things. We desperately need the Holy Spirit, and we need Him in power. We need His wisdom and His might and His fear and His worship and His counsel. When we have Him, we have all that is needed to be all that He desires us to be.

The Authority of the Son

This brings us to the authority of the eternal Son. About His authority three things are said: (1) He is the faithful witness, which means He is the prophet; (2) He is the first begotten of the dead, which means He is the priest; and (3) He is the prince of the kings of the earth, which means He is the king. When all of this is put together, the Lord Jesus Christ is Prophet, Priest and King, representing the threefold authority He has over all creation.

Jesus Christ was sent by the Father out of eternity into the world of time to bring us good news. This good news was that He was the prophet of all prophets, the summation of all the authority of all the prophets. In the Gospels, we find that Jesus Christ not only fulfilled prophecy in His teaching, but also His very deeds had prophetic meaning. In the strict sense of the word, Jesus Christ was the prophet in word and deed.

However, He was more than a prophet, He was the first begotten from the dead. He was the priest, and He was the only priest able to offer Himself to God as the final sacrifice. All other priests offered animals; but this priest, Christ, offered Himself. In the book of Hebrews, it says that He "through the eternal spirit offered himself without spot to God" (Heb. 9:14).

The only cross in all of history that was turned into an altar was the cross on which Jesus Christ died. It was a Roman cross. They nailed Him on it, and God, in His majesty and mystery, turned it into an altar. The Lamb who was dying in the mystery and wonder of God was turned into the Priest who offered Himself. No one else was a worthy offering.

Was there anybody living, in the day that Jesus died, who could have offered Jesus? No. In the days of Abraham, and all through the history of Israel, there were those who offered lambs. Only the priests and the high priest had that right. That is what they were supposed to do. The priest was superior to the lamb, so he took the lamb, cut its throat, poured its blood into a basin, sprinkled the people, sprinkled the book, and thus the lamb's blood became efficacious for the people.

As we come to this last Lamb, who is worthy to offer this Lamb that was above all priests, above all high priests and above all lambs and goats and all humans? This Lamb was above Melchisedec, and above Moses, and above Isaiah and David. Who could offer Him? Who was worthy? Nobody.

Then Jesus stepped forth and offered Himself. I believe with everything inside of me that a human being is at the right hand of God. A man is there—a glorified man—not a spirit, but a man. It is the resurrected Christ standing at the right hand of God the Father, exercising authority over His church.

One old Puritan preacher said, "Mankind has received the great dignity, that one of our number has been exalted to the right hand of the Majesty on high. One of our number has been exalted."

If my brother or my son were exalted to the presidency, I would be very happy about it and would say, "I have received a great dignity that one of my sons has become president of the United States." But we have received a dignity infinitely greater than the dignity of presidents and kings. We have received a dignity that one of our number has gone to a higher place than the president's office or a high priest's status. We honor these men, but there is a place above all. And that place is where Jesus Christ is. God has taken Him there, and He is there as our High Priest.

This Jesus Christ is the Prince of the Kings of the earth. He is the King of kings and Lord of lords over all the kingdoms and authorities of this earth. His authority is the final authority.

Both Benediction and Doxology

"Glory and dominion for ever and ever" (Rev. 1:6) is both the benediction and the doxology. It is a word of blessing and a word of praise. This puts all things in the right position—it is what true worship and praise do: "Grace and peace be unto you, and glory and dominion unto Him."

Imagine if that was reversed. Imagine if grace and peace be unto God and glory and dominion be unto you. What a terrible, grotesque and frightful situation we would be in if God needed grace and we got the glory and the dominion. But that can never be. "Grace and peace be unto you" is for you and me. What do we need more than grace? What more do we need for our wretched sinfulness than the grace of God? And what more do we need for our poor, uprooted, alienated, distraught souls than peace?

John's words "Unto him who loved us" (see Rev. 1:5) are the reason for all else, and yet love is not a thing of reason. Reason goes from point A to point B in a very logical manner. There is nothing logical or reasonable about love. Love rises above reason and logic but it does not contradict them. Who could imagine that the God who made the heavens and the earth and the sea and all things therein is condescending Himself to the form of a man? Out of His love, and dying for His people, it looks like an unreasonable thing to do from man's viewpoint. It was, however, reasonable in that it was the wisdom of the mighty God. Pure reason would have condemned us from the presence of God. His wisdom overruled the unreasonableness of His love for us.

Verse 5 continues, "Unto him that loved us, and washed us from our sins in his own blood," which He drew from His own veins and then made us kings and priests unto God. We do not hear much of this anymore. We often hear about the power and the authority of Christ, but rarely do we hear that Christ has declared unto us His authority. Here is the doctrine of the dominion of the saints.

I believe we have much greater dominion than we realize. I do not know whether you are afraid of the devil or not; but I, for one, do not have much fear for old Satan. I realize that he is the devil all right. I realize that he is a real devil and not simply a Santa Claus or a figment of human imagination. I believe in the personality and historicity of the devil. I believe the devil is an individual being. But I do not fear him, because I believe in the dominion and authority of the saints.

I believe God's people have authority in heaven. Here is the great delight of this truth: One of our number—Jesus—has been exalted to the right hand of the power on high. Think of Joseph, when he went down to Egypt and was seated on the throne. When his brothers came down to Egypt, he could get anything he wanted for them. They had authority because he had authority. They only had to go to Joseph and ask, and Joseph could give them their request. Joseph, one of their number, had been exalted to a place of authority. Because of their relationship to Joseph, they were beneficiaries of that authority.

When Jesus Christ our Lord went to the right hand of God, He went as one of the brethren. He sang among His brethren, said goodbye to them and went away to the right hand of God; and there He sits among His brethren. And He says to His brethren, "Anything you want, ask Me. Anything you want, you can have."

"Wait a minute," someone might inquire, "suppose God doesn't agree?" The answer is, God agrees because Jesus Christ is God as well as man. There is a unity in this authority based upon the unity of the Trinity. God is always God and will always act like God.

Joseph could get anything from Pharaoh for his brothers. That gave tremendous authority to Joseph and to Joseph's brethren. Just so, Christ can get anything for His people. I do not think there is any reason for us to hide and slink about as though apologizing for walking around on God's earth. I believe the boldest people in the world should be Christians—not cocky and sure of themselves, but sure of Him. I believe in the dominion and authority of the saints.

I also believe in the doctrine of the priesthood of all believers. You have a perfect right as a priest to go to the High Priest and make your wants and wishes known. When you do get what you want, you do so because you have great dignity in Christ. One of our number, one of our brethren, is at the right hand of God. Our connection to the throne and to the power and authority of that throne is in Jesus Christ, the God-man.

We walk on this earth with great power and authority because we live in the Blessed Hope of Jesus' coming again. Our authority is not in this world, but is rooted in heaven and in the One seated at the right hand of God the Father. Christianity is not about just sweating out our lives day by day; rather, it is about walking in the authority of heaven and looking unto Jesus, the author and finisher of our faith. Jesus Christ is about to return, and our life lived here below is in accordance with that great and mighty expectation. "Even so, come, Lord Jesus."

The Royal Priesthood
Gerhard Tersteegen (1697–1769)

The race of God's anointed priests
shall never pass away;
Before His glorious Face they stand,
and serve Him night and day.

Though reason raves, and unbelief flows on,
a mighty flood;
There are, and shall be, till the end,
the hidden priests of God.

His chosen souls, their earthly dross
consumed in sacred fire,
To God's own heart their hearts ascend
in flame of deep desire;

The incense of their worship fills
His Temple's holiest place;
Their song with wonder fills the Heavens,
the glad new song of grace.

4

THE SHINING LIGHT OF THE BLESSED HOPE

*O God our Father, we praise Thee for Thy Son, the Lord
Jesus Christ, who indeed is the Light of the world. We honor Thee
by honoring that Light which cometh into the world, which lighteth
every man that cometh into the world. May the glorious light
of the gospel shine through us in praise and honor of the
Shining Light of the Blessed Hope. Amen.*

The Blessed Hope is not just another doctrine to argue about and divide the fellowship. At the very core is the unveiling of the person of the Blessed Hope. God purposes that His churches should not themselves be the shining light, but that they should be the containers and receptacles of the shining light.

Three times in the first chapter of Revelation John identifies himself as the author. He says, "I, John, who also am your brother, and companion in tribulation, and in the kingdom and patience of Jesus Christ, was in the isle that is called Patmos, for the word of God, and for the testimony of Jesus Christ" (Rev. 1:9). He further tells us that he was in the spirit on the Lord's Day. It would be easy to get caught up in the theological minutia of what John meant by "The Lord's Day." That is not the purpose of what John has to say here. John was in a position to hear from God. His reason for being there was "for the Word of God and for the testimony of Jesus Christ."

"I was in the Spirit on the Lord's day," John writes, "and heard behind me a great voice, as of a trumpet" (v. 10). John turned to see what this voice was and saw the seven golden candlesticks. Those candlesticks, of course, were lampstands. They used candles in those days and stuck them in a candlestick. If you were well-to-do, you made golden candlesticks. A candle stuck in a candlestick illuminated the whole house.

Notice that it was not the candlesticks that shined. They were made of gold, but they were not shining. What were shining were the candles. And these seven golden candlesticks, Jesus explained, were the seven churches of Asia, and were meant to stand for all churches of all time. They did not shine, but they were the receptacle of all shining truth.

The Church is not to be a group of people who shine in society because of their social position or higher learning. Too many times, we have a candlestick trying to shine in lieu of the candle itself. It is not the business of any church to shine, nor is it our business to gather important people of whom everybody will say, "That church has a very high social standing." That is not the purpose of the local church.

I would rather go along with the church that did not have a very high social standing but had tremendous power. The apostle Peter did not have any academic degrees that I know of. He said to the lame beggar, "Silver and gold have I none; but such as I have give I thee: In the name of Jesus Christ of Nazareth rise up and walk" (Acts 3:6). He did not have much money, but when he said to the man, "Get up," the man got up.

The apostle John saw the seven golden candlesticks, which stand for all the churches that are the receptacles for all shining truth. Then he said, "In the midst of the candlesticks [I saw] one like unto the Son of man" (v. 13). That is the most important thing John saw.

A Portrait of the Resurrected Christ

If you understood that the candlesticks stood for the Church, whom would you expect to find standing in the midst of the seven churches? Would it be the apostle Paul? No, Paul died and may have even been dead when the book of Revelation was written. Who would you expect to be there? It was the one who said, "For where two or three are gathered together in my name, there am I in the midst of them" (Matt. 18:20).

Did He not also say, "Go ye into all the world, and preach the gospel to every creature" (Mark 16:15)? And, "Lo, I am with you always, even unto the end of the world" (Matt. 28:20)? You would expect the one who is standing in the midst of the Church to be the one of whom it was said was the Head of the Church, and "the fulness of Him that filleth all in all" (Eph. 1:23), the foundation upon which the Church is built. You would expect it to be Him who is the life of the Church.

Standing in the midst of the Church was one like unto the Son of Man. This was not a spirit; this was the Son of Man, Jesus Christ our Lord, clothed with a garment down to His feet.

Please make note of this chapter and meditate upon it often, because this is the only real portrait we have of the resurrected Christ. Many have painted portraits of Christ out of their own imaginations, but here is a visual image of the one standing in the midst of the churches in all His regal glory and majesty.

A Priestly Garment

John describes His clothing. First, John notices that He is clothed with a garment down to His feet, which is the priestly garment. We have here the priest in the midst of the church. Where else should a priest be?

Where were the priests in the Old Testament? They were in the midst of Israel. The Temple was in the midst of the camp; the holy place was in the midst of the Temple; and the priests were there, moving in and out. The high priest was in the holy place, and therefore was in the midst of Israel. Here is the Son of Man clothed with a garment down to His foot as a priest.

I believe in the priesthood. I believe in it in two ways. First, I believe in the priesthood of believers. You and I, as believers, are priests, and we have access to the throne of God through our High Priest, who has gone on before us. I also believe in the final, ultimate priesthood of our Lord Jesus Christ, who is the High Priest in the presence of God. John sees Him standing in the midst of His church in His priestly garments.

A Royal Insignia

Then John saw girt about His breast a golden girdle. This is the insignia of royalty. Around His chest was a broad band made of pure gold, and it held up the garment that went down to His feet. We see Him not as a spirit, not as an angel, not as a cherub, but as a man. You could have gone up to that man and touched Him. Jesus said to His disciples after the resurrection, "Behold my hands and my feet, that it is I myself: handle me, and see; for a spirit hath not flesh and bones, as ye see me have" (Luke 24:39). He ate fish in their presence. So this one that we have here in John's testimony is a true man. Not only is He a priest, but He is a royal priest—a priest who is both King and Priest.

The church used to talk more about Jesus as Prophet, Priest and King. Jesus Christ is all of these. We see Him here in Revelation 1 as all three combined: He is a kingly priest standing in the midst of His church, exercising His authority. This is why the true Church exists, and why it does not fall apart. With all the pressure the devil puts on the Church, how can the Church exist at all? I do not wonder that churches backslide; my wonder is that they do not all backslide. I do not wonder that churches do not hold together; the wonder is that they hold together at all.

If it were not for the invisible presence of our Lord in their midst—a Priest to stand before God for us, and a King to rule and exercise authority—there could be no church.

Hair as White as Snow

There are two prevailing views here, and I do not see why both cannot be true. Whenever I run into a passage where there are opposing views, my initial impulse is not to accept one and to reject the other. I try to see how they are interrelated. You get more out of truth that way, and you do not have to argue with anybody.

Some will say that Jesus Christ's pure whiteness means holiness. It is the utter holiness of our Lord that makes His hair to be whiter than wool. Others might say, no, it means right knowledge and solid judgment, and it is talking about the Ancient of Days. Because He is the Ancient of Days, dating back to time out of mind, we see Him as white-haired.

Maybe both views are true. On the other hand, I cannot quite believe that our Lord is gray-headed. I believe that our Lord has white hair, but it is not white because of age. His hair is white because He wanted to show us the utter holiness of the Lord. We are all but incapable of knowing what holiness is.

Here He is, white as wool, white as snow. This one who is standing in the midst of the churches is our holy Lord, and His head and His hair are white as wool. It is in His presence that we are going to live.

Eyes Like a Flame of Fire

You and I can see, but He sees all the way through. Like X-ray eyes, the eyes of our Lord are such that you cannot hide anything from Him. This one standing in the midst of the Church has those eyes, so there is not any use to clear your throat, swell out your chest and claim you are somebody. You are nobody, and I am nobody, and if we had our just desserts, we would all perish alike. He knows that and sees through it completely.

Some churches get so self-righteous. Like the Pharisees, they walk around trying to be the incarnated sum of all that is respectable. But they have no spirituality and no garment of righteousness to hide them from the flaming eyes of this one who stands in the midst of the Church. I would rather stand right out and be exactly what I am in His presence.

Feet Like Fine Brass

Feet like brass refers to the Judge who would judge what His eyes had just seen. The church that is not judged is not part of the church of the Lord Jesus Christ. Perhaps there are congregations meeting every Sunday that carry on programs and, for all practical truth, are not true churches of Jesus Christ at all.

The Spirit is not in the midst of them, and the Lord is not the center of their interest. They call themselves churches, but the true church is going to be a disciplined church; and our Priest in the midst of us, who knows all about us and loves us anyhow, is going to judge us. Never pray that the Lord should not judge you. Pray like the man David prayed in Psalm 38:1, if it is turned around and rightly translated: "Chastise me, O Lord, but not in thy wrath." The *King James Version* says, "Neither chasten me in thy hot displeasure." This leaves the impression that David did not want to be chastised. But David was praying that the Lord would chastise him not in anger, but in love.

A Voice Like the Sound of Many Waters

The fact that John wrote that the one who stood in the midst of the candlesticks, and who stands in the midst of the Church today, had a voice as the sound of many waters warms my heart and gives me a sense of something I cannot explain or express. The strong, majestic, deep voice of the One standing in the midst of the candlesticks . . . think what that voice has done!

That voice has called the worlds into being in the day when there was nothing. That voice called something, and it sprang into being. In the day when Lazarus was dead, that voice said, "Come forth, Lazarus," and Lazarus came forth. When that mighty voice said from the cross, "It is finished," the strong, bold soldiers of Caesar fell down and said in awe, "This indeed was the Son of God." That voice will someday wake the dead. That voice is the sound of many waters. You know that it is a musical sound.

We hear some big voices in our generation that raise the volume and boast of their importance. But there is one voice that will drown out all other voices. There is one voice with power and authority to do that with ease: the one who is standing in the midst of the golden candlesticks.

Seven Stars in His Hand

What are the seven stars? They are the messengers of the churches. They are those who go forth as messengers—as the angels of the churches. "Messenger" and "angel" are the same word, and they are held in the hand of the Lord Jesus.

I have always felt that it is too bad that churches divide on the question of the eternal security of believers. Some scream against it, and some scream in favor it. I stand in the middle and, thank God, I am in His hand. I can argue and write books on one side or the other, but I am going to say that I am in His hand. He holds His messengers in His hand. If you are a messenger, you are being held in His hand, and no person can take you out of His hand.

A Sharp Sword in His Mouth

All other words that come forth melt like butter in the hot sunshine; but the Word of the Lord, the sharp Sword of the Lord, will stand forever, impervious to its surroundings.

I wish I had known years back what the Lord has been teaching me lately. I used to preach a lot using examples from science, psychology and all the rest; but the Lord moved me away from that. Long before science and psychology ever reared their heads, the Word of the Lord was coming out of the mouth of the Man in the midst of the golden candlesticks and was like a sharp sword. We had better stay by the sharp Sword. I believe in the church that preaches the Word, the sharp Sword of the Spirit, for the Word of the Lord is like a sharp Sword that divides even to the marrow.

His Face Like the Sun Shining in Full Strength

There are descriptions of Jesus I can understand and appreciate, but here is the picture of Jesus I can understand best: "Behold my servant shall deal prudently, he shall be exalted and extolled, and be very high" (Isa. 52:13). I am asked to see that face again—that same face that once had spittle upon it; that face shining brighter than the sun in its full strength. You want to see how strong the sun is? Go look into the sky at noonday; you can never face the sun.

Scripture says that Jesus is "the image of the invisible God, the firstborn of every creature: For by him were all things created, that are in heaven, and that are in earth, visible and invisible, whether they be thrones, or dominions, or principalities, or powers: all things were created by him, and for him: And he is before all things, and by him all things consist" (Col. 1:15-17).

Some may object and say, "If He's in the midst, and He's like this, why can't we see Him?" That is the terrible part—He is in the midst, and we do not see Him. But I must not pass up remarking on the effect upon John of seeing Him. He fell at Jesus' feet as dead. Any real knowledge of Jesus Christ will knock all the pride out of a person and bring him or her down in lowliness before His feet. That is why I do not believe in this love song, romantic approach to Jesus Christ: "He's my lover, I'm his sweetheart." I do not believe in that kind of nonsense at all. It started in Hollywood, and it can stay there, as far as I am concerned. The one who has seen this One standing in the midst of the golden candlesticks will fall down before Him in silence and absolute worship and adoration.

Our Only Possible Response

Seeing this one that was in the midst of the seven golden candlesticks had a terrible effect upon John. "When I saw him," John writes, "I fell at his feet as dead" (Rev. 1:17). The man who has never fallen at the feet of Jesus in astonished wonder has never been able to get up and move a congregation by preaching about Jesus. But John did. Immediately, John testifies, "He laid his right hand upon me, saying unto me, Fear not; I am the first and the last: I am he that liveth, and was dead; and, behold, I am alive for evermore, Amen; and have the keys of hell and of death" (vv. 17-18).

Whoever was it that came up with the idea that Peter had the keys? I see Jesus Christ standing in the midst of His church and swinging a set of keys—iron keys and golden keys. Iron keys will unlock the brazen gates of hell, and the golden keys will unlock the glorious gates of heaven. And Jesus alone has those keys.

The most important thing about the Church is the one who is in the midst. He is here to see and to judge. He is here to keep us and represent us to God, and represent God to us. He is here to speak, to reprove and to encourage us. Why don't we see Him? How terrible it is to play in His presence, to dream in His presence, to sleep in His presence, to sin in His presence. How terrible! He is coming again in glory. In the meantime, He is holding His Church together, getting His Church ready. That is what we are here for. We are here to get ready. We are in the grand parade, preparing for Jesus' return.

The place where the Church gets ready is a battlefield. It is a place where there is sin and woe. The Bride has to get ready in the midst of warfare and her labors; but she must get ready. That is why you were not immediately transferred to heaven when you were born again. When you were saved, you got a new nature, and that nature belongs with God; but you were not taken to God, because you were not ready. He is getting you ready now. You are being prepared as a Bride, as a purified people; you are getting ready. Do not let anybody talk you out of that.

As the book of Revelation develops, it tells us about future events. The unveiling of the Christ of Revelation creates what we call the Blessed Hope. Everything else pales to insignificance in comparison to this one great truth: Jesus is coming.

O Quickly Come, Dread Judge of All
Lawrence Tuttiett (1825–1897)

O quickly come, dread Judge of all;
For, awful though Thine advent be,
All shadows from the truth will fall,
And falsehood die, in sight of Thee;
O quickly come, for doubt and fear
Like clouds dissolve when Thou art near.

O quickly come, great King of all;
Reign all around us, and within;
Let sin no more our souls enthrall,
Let pain and sorrow die with sin;
O quickly come, for Thou alone
Canst make Thy scattered people one.

O quickly come, true Life of all;
For death is mighty all around;
On every home his shadows fall,
On every heart his mark is found.
O quickly come, for grief and pain
Can never cloud Thy glorious reign.

O quickly come, sure Light of all;
For gloomy night broods o'er our way;
and weakly souls begin to fall
With weary watching for the day.
O quickly come, for round Thy throne
No eye is blind, no night is known.

5

THE DIVINE IMPERATIVE OF THE BLESSED HOPE

O God, our heavenly Father, we have searched and failed to find anybody worthy to reign over heaven above and earth below save Thy Son, even the Lord Jesus Christ. Thy Scriptures declare Him the only praiseworthy one. My worshiping heart recognizes and declares Him to reign supreme in my life. May I so live each day as to honor His sovereignty in my life. Amen.

What amazes me with the whole scene of Bible prophecy is that so many people today think they know more about it than Daniel and John the Revelator. They present their views in such a way that you must take what they say without questioning it. If you do not believe what they say, you are accused of not being a fundamentalist.

I could explore many reasons why Bible prophecy has taken such a beating. Instead of that, let me merely set forth the plain teaching of the Scriptures. Psalm 2:1-9 and 1 Corinthians 15:25-28, and other Scriptures we could examine, show that Jesus Christ is going to reign. In 1 Corinthians 15:26, Paul points to a complete universal redemption in the future, stating, "The last enemy that shall be destroyed is death." To abolish death, Christ must reign.

Let's consider the qualifications necessary for this Reigning One and why Jesus Christ alone fits those qualifications.

Why We Need the Reigning One

All we need to do is look at world politics today and see the confusion and lack of anything resembling unity around the world. Politicians pontificate about how they are going to solve the problems, but none are being solved. With this in mind, I believe there are six reasons why this Reigning One is required. The world in general has six major problems that must be solved.

First, *the weak must be delivered from the opposition of the strong.* Psalm 72 teaches this very clearly and is only a sampling of what the Bible teaches about a time coming when the oppressed people shall go free and the weak shall be delivered from the strong. The Reigning One must so deliver the weak.

Second, *the human race must be rescued from the tyranny of what we call sin.* Sin is not only a crime that man commits against God; it is also a monster that rides humanity to exhaustion. All through the Bible, we are taught that the human race must be delivered from this tyrant, and man cannot free himself.

Third, *Israel must be delivered from her ancient tormentors.* I wonder if we can ever hope for that while Satan roams loose in the earth and Israel is at the mercy of her Gentile neighbors. Will she ever be delivered from her ancient tormentors? Yes, the Scriptures tell us this will take place. Who will be the one to step forward and deliver Israel from her tormentors?

Fourth, *the world must have a perfect leader.* The problems of the world today have developed beyond any human solution, and no human has the power to solve these problems. Certainly, humans have created the problems through their sin and disobedience, but no human has stepped forward who can deliver the world. Up to this point in history, everyone who has tried has failed.

Fifth, *the evil spiritual powers must have a master, and death must have an executioner.* The phrase from the old Welsh song "Guide Me, O Thou Great Jehovah" puts this in the proper perspective:

Death of death, and hell's destruction,
Land me safe on Canaan's side.

This being true, Jesus Christ must be the executioner of death, which has not happened yet. Only He can rule over death and completely master those evil spiritual powers that wreak such havoc in our world today.

Sixth, *death must have an executioner.* As it stands now, death rules. Only Jesus Christ is able to defeat death. He put it all under His feet in a final stance of victory. In order to deliver the weak from the oppression of the strong, and the human race from the tyranny of sin, and Israel from her ancient tormentors, and the world from her problems, and to thus have a perfect leader, we must have someone with certain and specific qualifications.

The Qualifications of the Reigning One

The qualification of the world leader that is coming is rather specific. Let me lay before you several of these considerations.

A Native of the Earth

First, *the one who brings about this wondrous golden age must be a native of the earth.* The human race is inextricably united with the earth. We are sons of the earth whether we like it or not. We are born in a sanitary hospital, walk around on sidewalks most of our lives, die again in the hospital two floors down, and then are put away in Memorial Park without any sign of death. In spite of the fact, we are still an earthy people. For the earth is our mother. From her we took the very body we have. This earth we live in provides us with nourishment for our bodies. This is our home, this earth, and apart from sin and death, I have not a thing against the earth. Truly it is from dust to dust.

The earth is our home and will finally be our grave. The earth calls us back to her arms again and we lie down and sleep in the bosom of the same earth from which we sprang. That earth, in the meantime, has been our battleground, our playground, our field, our home, our all in all, as far as this life is concerned.

Then, God, who is going to bring peace to the earth, is going to have to have somebody who qualifies as belonging to the earth. He could not send an archangel to reign. If the archangel Gabriel were to come down to Washington, he would not know what to say, except that the Lord has instructed him. He would have no sympathy to all of the earth. He was not born here. He is spirit, not flesh. He knows nothing about being born, growing up in school, stubbing your toe and getting the measles. He knows nothing about the troubles we go through down here; but Jesus our Lord knew, and that one who comes must be able to say, "I am of the earth. I was born here in the earth."

God will not send us a stranger, somebody coming in from outside telling us how to solve our problems. They would not know anything about our problems. Personally, I do not want somebody coming from London or Washington to try to run the United States, and neither would you want somebody to come from Washington and try to run your town. We do not want any archangels or cherubim down here to this earth where we stumble along in the darkness and watch the sun rise and the moon come up. We want somebody who knows our people, who knows us as human beings, who knows us—red and yellow, black and white—all around the world.

We need somebody who has been tempted in all points, like we are, and yet without sin. We need somebody who bears our body and looks like us, and that one, of course, is Jesus Christ, our Lord. He is someone who fully identifies with our human plight and we can feel comfortable trusting Him.

Jesus Christ is the Son of man, and He is the native of the earth. Keep in mind that He is God and was before the earth was. He was with God in the beginning, and He created all things. He also made the same earth that was His birthplace, His playground, the place of His crucifixion and the place of His resurrection. He is a man of the earth; He knows the earth and He knows earth's people.

In the Old Testament, the high priest was taken from among the Jewish people in order that they might know the people. Jesus Christ was born among us that He might know and understand us. He received His body from the earth. He walked on the earth and drank of the water of the earth. He rode on her lakes and walked on the highways. He washed the dust of her lanes off His feet. He lay down to sleep on her bosom at night; and when He was dead, they tucked Him away in a quiet place in her bosom, from which God raised Him the third day, according to the Scriptures.

Jesus Christ is part of the earth, and He is of the stock of which the earth and the world and humanity are made. An archangel could never claim that. Not even a cherubim could claim that. No strange creature from any other planet could claim that. However, Jesus Christ, He is a man, and He is one of us.

Unspotted Holiness

Second, *the one to reign must have unspotted holiness.* A holy God must have a holy King. Jesus Christ is the Holy One of God. The enemies of the ages have found no spot in Him. Even the fiercest and severest enemies of Christianity bow their heads in silence when the name of Jesus comes up because they know He was a holy man. Even the devil had to flee from His presence and His enemies admit that this man was surely the Son of God.

Unchallenged Right to Reign

Third, *the one to reign must have an unchallenged right to reign.* This Jesus Christ, our Lord, is both God and man, and so He can reign, for God rules over man. He is the only one in the universe who can do that. If somebody had merely been a man, he could not reign for God over us because he would not understand God's side. If he had been God only, he could not reign because we could say, "How does God know our problems?" Jesus Christ is both God and man; and so as God, He reigns over humanity, because He Himself is man and knows both God and man.

Jesus Christ came in line with the ancient Scriptures. Two thousand years of scriptural prophecy had gone ahead of Jesus Christ our Lord. Those predictions were so minute and so detailed that nobody else in the world could possibly fulfill them. Nobody could mistake Him; no one else could establish this claim based upon the prophecies of Scripture. These prophecies said that He would be born at a certain time, in a certain place, of a certain line, of a certain race, of a certain family. When Jesus came, He came born of that line, that race, that family, that place and approximately at that time. Nobody else can claim that.

Buddha could not make such a claim; he came too soon. Mohammad could not make that claim; he came too late. The genealogical tablets in Israel were kept up until the time Christ was born. Every family registered their baby boys when they were born so they could trace their lineage all the way back to Abraham. Everybody knew what line the Messiah would come from. A few years after Christ was born, Titus (AD 30–81) came and destroyed the city, and now nobody knows where those tablets are. You cannot prove that you belong to any particular tribe; therefore, nobody can come along and say, "I am the Messiah." That was fulfilled in Jesus Christ the Lord. He has unchallenged right to claim that He is the one about whom God spoke in the Old Testament prophecies.

Faithful to Man and to God

Fourth, *the one who reigns has to be faithful, both to man and to God.* As a man and as God, He can reign as God over man without making compromising concessions. The Scripture says He must reign. Of the details, I am going to leave to those who know more about it than I do. I am at the place in my life where I believe more strongly in the coming of Christ than I ever did in my life, but I have less dogmatic views of the details. I believe there is a Reigning One coming. I believe that God will give Him the nations of the earth and He will reign and rule over them. He will right whatever is wrong. He will reign in righteousness, bring peace, judge the poor, break in pieces the oppressor and have dominion over all the earth. He will deliver the needy when He comes and redeem the souls of the people from deceit and violence.

The earth, as we know it, is full of riddles yet to be solved. From my study of Scripture, it is in my opinion that Christ must reign until each one of those riddles has been solved to His honor and glory. Not long ago, everyone who thought they knew everything taught that we could all get together and everybody would love everybody else. It would be that simple. In actuality, there is more hatred today than since the beginning of the world. Perhaps there has never been a time in human history when people say meaner, nastier, more abusive and horrible things about other people than they do now. This is the day when they have cast God's cord from them and broken His bands asunder, and the nations have tumultuously assembled and imagined vain things.

I do not enjoy bringing up unpleasant things, but after all, we are immersed in racial antagonism. It is all over the world. No matter where you go in this world, there is racial hatred, which really does not make sense. If you have less or more pigmentation than I have, you are going to be suspicious of me. If your nose is shaped differently from mine or your eyes slant otherwise, we are going to stand and glare at each other across imaginary lines. Racial antagonism will continue until the Reigning One comes.

What about economics? I am not an expert on economics. I am not alone here; few people know anything about it either. I know how to change dollars into dimes and make out my taxes, but that is about as far as I go in the area of economics. The way the world is going, nobody else knows much about economics either.

Then there is disease. We are told that diseases are being conquered, but every time we conquer one, another disease breaks out. The highest standards in the world are on the North American continent, but we eat more fat than all the other countries in the world put together and we have more heart attacks. It seems medical experts get one thing whipped and another one comes along just as deadly. One problem solved, two more take its place.

Somebody must come who knows something about this; and I do not know where to look for him among men. No genius has ever been equal to these problems of how to handle world politics, how to make people love each other, how to keep peace in the world, how to settle racial antagonism so that people of different colors and shapes don't give in to hatred and try to kill each other. We need somebody to solve the economic problems so there are no more strikes, wars and people being beaten up. We need somebody who knows how to solve the disease problem so we can walk around on the earth without diseases. Presently, no genius has ever been equal to this. Nobody can claim this position.

Heart, Knowledge and Power

How are these problems going to be solved? First, you have to have a heart that wants to do it. We have in our world today lack of heart, a lack of love for humanity. Second, you must have the knowledge of how to do it. Nobody seems to know how to do these things. Third, you must have the power to do it. This, of course, emphasizes the lack of our power to accomplish this.

In all three of these things—love, knowledge and power—only Jesus Christ fits. He has a love for humanity in unlimited abundance. His wisdom is unlimited; and the Scripture says, "All power is given unto me" (Matt. 28:18). In all of these areas, Jesus Christ fits supremely. Nobody else does. Nobody else comes close.

When Jesus Christ came into the world, He had the infinite compassion of God, for He is God. All the infinite compassion of God was in His heart, and He never looked at a blind man without grief and sorrow in His heart. He never looked at a deaf man who was unable to hear the sweet sounds of nature without grief in His heart. He never looked at a man with a withered hand or a crippled leg, or a dead girl being carried out on a bier, without sorrow in His heart. He loved people, not populations; He loved people. He loved the look of them and the sound of them and the warmth of them and the eyes of them. Jesus loved people and loved them so much that He gave everything He had for them. He had the heart to do it.

None of the leaders of the world today has a heart big enough to want to bring peace and prosperity to the world. This Reigning One must have the wisdom to know how to do it. Only one person fits this description. There is only one person who is wisdom and righteousness and in whom all wisdom is hidden away. He knows all the answers and would never have to say, "Excuse me, I don't know." He has all the knowledge of God. This One is coming to reign; and when He comes, He will know instantly how to solve the economic problems, the political problems, the racial problems, the physical problems of the world. He will solve them because He is God, and He became flesh to dwell among us.

He must reign until the riddles of the world are solved, and He must reign until evil is put down forever. Only Christ has this power. All others who have come before had a certain amount of power, but even the best of them died. Some of them died before they could even finish what needed to be done. But this One who is to come, Jesus Christ, not only has the power, but He has also destroyed and defeated death, once and for all. This Reigning One is the resurrected Christ upon whom death no more has dominion.

Because of this, He will abolish death. Nobody has been able to do that. Only two men in the world ever escaped death:

Elijah was one and Enoch the other (see Gen. 5:24; 2 Kings 2:11). They both escaped death because God allowed it; but apart from these two, death has reigned since the beginning of time. This terrible thing called death reigns over all the earth, and nobody has ever been able to escape it. Now this One who comes, this Reigning One, this resurrected Christ has abolished death and put it under His foot.

Now death reigns; we die. But the Scriptures say He must reign. He must reign until death is defeated. He won that victory over death by paying a debt He did not owe. He paid a debt nobody could ever properly claim He owed, and this brought into His hands the power finally to reign over death.

The apostle Paul wrote, "He must reign, till he hath put all enemies under his feet. The last enemy that shall be destroyed is death" (1 Cor. 15:25-26). This is why I believe Christ is coming back to the world again. This is why I believe that Jesus Christ must reign: because He is the only One in the universe with the proper qualifications for it. He is the only One who has a heart big enough to want to do it, the wisdom infinite enough to do it and sufficient power to be able to do it. He is the only One who has the unchallenged right, according to the prophetic Scriptures. He is the only One who is a native of the earth, and as a native of the earth and a member of the human race, He has the unchallenged right to reign over the human race. He is the only One qualified to reign.

I believe He is coming to earth again to reign, and I am glad to leave the details with those who know more about it than I do. But I am gazing upward with the Blessed Hope. I do not see how it can be very much longer. Maybe there are things I do not know. Maybe He will tarry longer. If He does, I do not know how we are going to get on, because we are so busy trying to destroy ourselves. He who is the Reigning One will soon come.

Jesus Shall Reign
Isaac Watts (1674–1748)

Jesus shall reign where'er the sun
Doth his successive journeys run;
His kingdom stretch from shore to shore,
Till moons shall wax and wane no more.

Behold the islands with their kings,
And Europe her best tribute brings;
From north to south the princes meet,
To pay their homage at His feet.

There Persia, glorious to behold,
There India shines in eastern gold;
And barb'rous nations at His word
Submit, and bow, and own their Lord.

To Him shall endless prayer be made,
And praises throng to crown His head;
His Name like sweet perfume shall rise
With every morning sacrifice.

People and realms of every tongue
Dwell on His love with sweetest song;
And infant voices shall proclaim
Their early blessings on His Name.

Blessings abound wherever He reigns;
The prisoner leaps to lose his chains;
The weary find eternal rest,
And all the sons of want are blessed.

Where He displays His healing power,
Death and the curse are known no more:
In Him the tribes of Adam boast
More blessings than their father lost.

Let every creature rise and bring
Peculiar honors to our King;
Angels descend with songs again,
And earth repeat the loud amen!

Great God, whose universal sway
The known and unknown worlds obey,
Now give the kingdom to Thy Son,
Extend His power, exalt His throne.

The scepter well becomes His hands;
All Heav'n submits to His commands;
His justice shall avenge the poor,
And pride and rage prevail no more.

With power He vindicates the just,
And treads th'oppressor in the dust:
His worship and His fear shall last
Till hours, and years, and time be past.

As rain on meadows newly mown,
So shall He send his influence down:
His grace on fainting souls distills,
Like heav'nly dew on thirsty hills.

The heathen lands, that lie beneath
The shades of overspreading death,

Revive at His first dawning light;
And deserts blossom at the sight.

The saints shall flourish in His days,
Dressed in the robes of joy and praise;
Peace, like a river, from His throne
Shall flow to nations yet unknown.

6

The Glorious Sign of the Blessed Hope

*Our Heavenly Father, as we pierce the mystery surrounding Thy
throne in heaven, language fails us in describing Thy glory.
We bow in silent wonder and amazement as we seek to focus on Thee.
What our mind cannot comprehend our heart leaps up in
worshipful adoration of Thy revelation. Amen.*

Throughout the entire created universe, there are only two substances: that which is God and that which is not God. That which is God is spiritual, unique, uncreated, unapproachable, incomprehensible and wholly other than. It is super-rational and super-sensible and escapes all our efforts to get at Him. Yet if we are humble, it will come to us. We can never rise high enough to greet Him; He has condescended to our level, through the gospel, to greet us and to meet us.

Then there is that which is not God—all that God has created. It is not eternal; rather, it is finite. It is made and is merely the handiwork of God, and it is what we are most familiar with. David, the psalmist said, "The heavens declare the glory of God; and the firmament showeth his handywork" (Ps. 19:1). Many have become experts in the "handywork" of God, but they have never pierced through the mystery of knowing God personally. We can see what God has done, but we come far short of knowing the one who has created all things.

In the opening verses of Revelation 4, John looked through an open door and saw "a throne was set in heaven, and one that sat on the throne" (v. 2). John does not identify the one who sat on the throne. But from the context, we know who that was. When prophecy teachers try to give us a picture of the world to come, they are not puzzled because things are not clear, but because they are too clear. They are seeing things the like of which they have never seen before, and so they have to tell us what these things are like. They are not like anything exactly, but they are somewhat like it, and there is our problem. They are trying to describe and define in human terms that which eludes man's language.

In this picture of the one on the throne, we see that God wants to disclose Himself to John. In the Old Testament, Moses took the protection of a rock to be safe from the face of God; but here was God coming out, and yet not really coming out. Here was God being seen, and yet not quite being seen. In describing what he saw, John lacked the language and the ideas to replicate the experience. When he looked at the one on the throne, his eyes could not focus on God. If he had focused on God, he would have gone blind.

When Moses' desire was to see God's face, God said, "Thou canst not see my face: for there shall no man see me, and live" (Exod. 33:20). In spite of Moses' desire, he could not cross a line. His passion for God launched him as far as he could go in God's direction. God, in His graciousness, stopped Moses short and placed him in the cleft of a rock.

As John looks through the open door, he is discovering God's passion to reveal Himself. How can the infinite receive the finite, or the finite the infinite? The Infinite One, the one who has no bounds, was to be received by the one who has bounds. God is wholly other than. He is beyond and elevated and transcendent.

A definite difference exists between the evangelical mystics and the evangelical rationalists. An evangelical mystic like John stands in the presence of the awesome God and cries, "Holy, holy, holy," and falls down at His feet as dead. The evangelical rationalist figures it all out and says, "We can understand it; we know how it is," then writes a long, learned book about it, describing exactly what it is like.

The evangelical rationalists are trying to educate themselves out of the miry pit, but they will never fully get out. God will never allow man, while the world stands, to think his way out of this horrible pit. You are going to have to have an open vision, an open door, an illuminated heart; and then you are going to have to stand, looking through that open door at that awesome throne, saying, "Oh, Lord God, is it I?"

God Comes to Man

That which is not God and that which is God are separated. Because I understand this, it does not mean that I can understand God. God has revealed Himself sometimes in what the theologians call a theophany, which is the setting forth of the shining of God. What we know about God is what God has deliberately revealed to us about Himself.

God has revealed Himself by figure, similitude and many like images; by angels and by fire He has made Himself known to man. He has come and revealed Himself in theophanies. Those were only theophanies, of course, when God revealed Himself as fire and was in Israel as fire. It was God, and it was not God; for God is not fire. The Bible says that God is a consuming fire, and yet it does not mean God is that which flames up from a match when you strike it. Unfortunately, there are those who believe that comparison is literal. When God said He is a flaming fire, He does not mean that literally. When I strike a match and hold it up, and it flickers and then goes out, that is not God. It is not God, but it is like God, and it is that which is a mysterious and fiery substance such as God is.

Another theophany happened when the angels came down to the city of Sodom. God said, "I'll go down and see." The angels go down to see whether things are as bad as they say they are. Immediately, there were two angels talking to Abraham. Those two angels were a revelation, undoubtedly, of the Father and the Son, because God said, "I'll go down." When He appeared, there were two men. Sometimes it is a man; and sometimes it is an angel; and sometimes it is fire; but God appears.

Revelations in the Throne Room

As John looked at the throne and the one seated on the throne, he also saw a rainbow. That rainbow is interesting. A rainbow is, of course, what you see in the day of storm, and God made that rainbow to be a sign of a covenant and of protection eternally. God said, "One time I destroyed the world by flood, but the next time it'll be by fire, and that will be at the end of things. In the meantime, don't worry about floods." The rainbow around the throne was a sign of God's covenant, the sign of eternal protection. The world will not be destroyed by water again, but by fire. This rainbow went all the way around the throne, as if to say, here is a covenant protection all the way around. This protection included and embraced the elders sitting clothed in white raiment, the beasts that were there—the strange creatures, the 24 elders. They were all there, and around about them went this circle, and there was not a spot where the devil could get in.

The 24 elders around the throne are significant. For whom do they stand? Here again would be a place to become divided. There should be no division over things that do not matter. If a man insists he does not believe the Scripture, I can shake hands with him and live in the same town without having trouble. I am not, however, going to kneel and pray with him, or go to church with him, if he does not believe the Word of God. There can be a division that does us good, and then there can be a division that does us harm.

Who are these 24 elders? I think they stand for the overcomers of both Israel and the Church. I think they go back and stand for all the overcomers of the 12 tribes of Israel and the 12 apostles of the Lamb. Notice what Scripture reveals in Matthew 19:27-28:

> Then answered Peter and said unto him, Behold, we have forsaken all, and followed thee; what shall we have therefore? And Jesus said unto them, Verily I say unto you, That ye which have followed me, in the regeneration when the Son of man shall sit in the throne of his glory, ye also shall sit upon twelve thrones, judging the twelve tribes of Israel.

Surrounding the throne were lightning and thunder and voices and the seven fires. God and His throne are unchanged, but the cup of iniquity on earth is filling up. I am not at all worried about my relation to God or about the fact that the sovereign God will have His way in the whirlwind and the storm; the day will come when there will be peace and that which men now talk about and do not believe in. There will be that time when there will be peace from the river to the ends of the earth.

Yet, I am worried, because when the cup of iniquity fills up, then the judgment of God comes. I only hope that we will not be here when the judgment of God comes down upon this terrible earth. I do not want to be on earth during that time when God rises up to shake the earth and the nations. If the holy justice of God will be able to stand it much longer, it will be a wonder. We have sinned and forfeited away all right we might have ever had to the protection of God. The cup of iniquity is fast filling up, and when it reaches its limit, God's judgment will fall.

These lightnings, thunderings and voices are going to come and sound out in that day when the cup of the earth has been filled up. When the justice of God has been violated so long, so consistently and so arrogantly that He will not take it anymore, then lightnings and thunderings shall go out from the throne. The throne of grace will become a throne of judgment.

Creatures Around the Throne

John saw the creatures around the throne. The first living creature was like a lion; the second was like a calf; the third had the face of a man; and the fourth living creature was like a flying eagle; these are the four beasts, or four living creatures.

The Face of a Lion

The creature or beast with the face of a lion represents the kingship of Jesus Christ the Lord. The kingly idea is a noble idea, because the glory of the king does not lie so much in the person of the king as much as it lies in the person of the people. When you look at a king or a queen, you don't mind calling them all sorts of "your Majesty" and "your noble" this and that, because you know these addresses do not mean the person they are talking about, but everybody over whom they reign. So the king idea is a noble idea, for the glory of the king lies in the freedom and the happiness of his people. The glory of Jesus Christ, the Lion, lies in the fact that He is the ruler over people who will be supremely and perfectly happy throughout the entire universe.

The Face of the Calf
What is a calf doing there? It is obedience unto sacrifice. The little calf that did not have much on his side, did not have much to look forward to but death and blood and sacrifice, was there. God had Him there—the Calf and the Lamb.

The Face of a Man
This represents the manhood of Jesus Christ. He came into this world as the God-man. He was both God and man, of which the theologians call the hypostatic union. It was the man Jesus who hung on the cross and died for the sins of the world. It is the man Jesus who now is representing us at the right hand of God the Father. Therefore, our connection with the throne is this man Jesus Christ.

The Face of the Flying Eagle
This represents the deity of Jesus Christ. Yes, He was a God, but He was the God-man. As man, He represents us before the throne; and as God, He represents the throne before man. He brings us together in absolute union.

Unceasing Worship

One thing that catches my attention in this scene of the throne is the unceasing worship. Notice that the elders and the creatures were united in response. The beasts gave glory and honor first. Each of them had six wings, and they were full of eyes within, and they rested not day and night, saying, "Holy, holy, holy." And yet we are so tolerant of ourselves that we believe a man who has never said, "Holy, holy, holy" and meant it, who would consider himself bored to tears if he had to dwell day and night in heaven crying, "Holy, holy, holy," we would preach him right off into heaven as soon as he dies, and say, "He's gone into heaven." Now, would such a person be fit for the atmosphere of worship in heaven? When those beasts gave glory and honor and thanks to Him that sits on the throne, who lives forever and ever, it stirred up the elders.

One nice thing about great hymn singing, it stirs up someone else to worship. When the four beasts worshiped, then the four elders woke up and said, "Let us worship," and down they went on their knees before Him that sat on the throne, and they worshiped Him that liveth forever and ever and cast their crowns before Him, crying, "Thou art worthy, O Lord." This is not Jesus they are talking about now. This is God, the Father. "Thou art worthy, O Lord, to receive glory and honour and power: for thou hast created all things, and for thy pleasure they are and were created" (Rev. 4:11).

Those ascriptions of praise to the Father and the casting of the crowns at His holy feet are preliminary to the opening of the seals on the scrolls. While I stand on this earth there exist out of my sight but in reality, the throne, and one on the throne, and the rainbow around the throne, circling in everlasting covenant protection. There exist around the throne the representatives of the creatures who never fell and the representatives of the creatures who fell and were redeemed. There is a third classification of creatures not represented here. They are the creatures that fell and were not redeemed and will never be redeemed.

The first two classes are found here around the throne—those who never fell and those who fell and were redeemed. But the third terrible class is not found here. They are found elsewhere, but we know they are not here. We know they are in the sight of God, because there are lightnings, thunderings, voices and fires, and God is getting ready to send His judgment upon them.

Why God Allows Us to See His Throne

A divine purpose rests on this awesome revelation. It has been revealed so that the wise and the believing live in the light of it. Then these things are revealed that the foolish and unbelieving may stand without excuse.

The apostle Paul experienced shipwreck out in the Mediterranean one terrible night. The ship broke to pieces and everybody finally got ashore. Some came to shore on boards, and some on oars, and some on bits of floating cargo and some on this and some on that, but they all got to shore. Therefore, you do not have to know everything. You only have to know that you are a sinner, Christ died for you and that if you will believe on Christ, you will be saved. You are a Christian who is all mixed up, as you say, but you do not have to be. You can come back on any verse that will bring you in, even on some verses some people do not believe are for you.

There is a great, overwhelming philosophy of the world that we were brought into the world with a design, with an ending. I want you to justify your existence. I want you to tell me what right you have to live. I want you to excuse yourself before the bar of God and the judgment of humanity.

Who is to be blamed if we miss this? Who is to be blamed if we miss salvation, and the privilege of standing with these for whom the 24 elders stand, the creatures, those redeemed souls we read about later in the book of Revelation? If I miss this, then it would be far better that I had been carried from my mother's arms to the grave when I was yet an unnamed infant. Far better for me that I should never have breathed God's fresh air and basked in God's sunshine. Far better that I should have never gone to Sunday School as a young person and heard, "God is love, for God died for the ungodly." Far better that I should never have heard it.

If I miss it, whom can I blame? Certainly not the God who sits on the throne; certainly not the Lamb who stands before the throne like as He had been slain; certainly not the fiery Holy Ghost that leaps out all over the world bringing the gospel to men. If, after all I have done in living my life and following my own pleasures, with all of the struggles in all of the hardships . . . if I miss this, was it really worth my struggle? Can I blame the One who condescended to my level to rescue me from the detriment of my sin? Was my rebellion against God really worth it?

Lo! What a Glorious Sight Appears
Isaac Watts (1674–1748)

Lo! What a glorious sight appears
To our believing eyes!
The earth and seas are passed away,
And the old rolling skies.

From the third heav'n, where God resides,
That holy, happy place,
The New Jerusalem comes down,
Adorned with shining grace.

Attending angels shout for joy,
And the bright armies sing—
"Mortals! behold the sacred seat
Of your descending King.

"The God of glory down to men
Removes His blest abode;
Men, the dear objects of His grace,
And he the loving God.

"His own soft hand shall wipe the tears
From every weeping eye,
And pains, and groans, and griefs, and fears,
And death itself, shall die."

How long, dear Savior! O, how long
Shall this bright hour delay?
Fly swifter round, ye wheels of time,
And bring the welcome day.

7

THE MYSTIC SHROUD OF THE BLESSED HOPE

O Lord, our God, we adore Thee and the splendor of Thy revelations. Thou hast bid me to seek Thy face, and in great fear and trepidation, I seek Thy face. My eyes long to see Thee but Thy holiness constrains me. I must see Thee; when shall I come and appear before Thee? I turn my back on all others and seek only Thee and the fullness of Thy revelation. Amen.

In reflecting upon the throne and the one sitting thereon, I cannot help but see the cloud concealing Him from us. When referring to our Lord, the mention of a cloud is rather important. When He went away, He went away in a cloud. This has nothing whatsoever to do with clouds that we are so familiar with today that bring the rain. God would never hide Himself in such a cloud. When our Lord went away, He went away in another kind of cloud, and it is important for us to understand the significance of the cloud. It is the cloud of the Shekinah—the cloud of the Presence. It is simply the Mystic Shroud of God's impenetrable presence.

This cloud has a glorious and wondrous history throughout the Bible. It is often referred to as the Shekinah glory of God. God conceals Himself from the eyes of unredeemed men and women and will only give flashes of illumination to those who have been born again and those who long to see the face of God. David often prayed to see the face of God.

> Hide not thy face far from me; put not thy servant away in anger: thou hast been my help; leave me not, neither forsake me, O God of my salvation (Ps. 27:9).

> Turn us again, O God of hosts, and cause thy face to shine; and we shall be saved (Ps. 80:7).

David would settle for nothing short of the face of God. Our problem today is that we usually settle for anything and everything but that shining face of God. The cost and inconvenience of pressing deep into His presence are too much for the kind of life we are living. History abounds with references to this Mystic Cloud concealing the presence of Almighty God.

The Cloud of God's Presence

A quick review of Bible history gives some indication of what this cloud is all about. When Israel came out of Egypt and crossed the Red Sea into the wilderness, she had a cloud over her, and in that cloud dwelt the mighty Shekinah of the presence of God. The cloud ruled by day, and a pillar of fire ruled by night. It was the same Presence by day as by night.

The cloud served two purposes. First, it protected Israel from her enemy. No enemy could touch Israel without the direct permission of Jehovah. Time and time again, we see this very truth illustrated for us throughout the history of Israel, particularly in the wilderness. In order for an enemy to touch Israel in any way, that enemy had to penetrate that which is impenetrable, the presence of Jehovah, the Shekinah glory.

Second, this cloud concealed His face from Israel while still leading them. Moses, in the spirit of faith, challenged God to show Himself:

> And Moses said unto the LORD, See, thou sayest unto me, Bring up this people: and thou hast not let me know whom thou wilt send with me. Yet thou hast said, I know thee by name, and thou hast also found grace in my sight. Now therefore, I pray thee, if I have found grace in thy sight, show me now thy way, that I may know thee, that I may find grace in thy sight: and consider that this nation is thy people. And he said, My presence shall go with thee, and I will give thee rest. And he said unto him, If thy presence go not with me, carry us not up hence. For wherein shall it be known here that I and thy people have found grace in thy sight? is it not in that thou goest with us? so shall we be separated, I and thy people, from all the people that are upon the face of the earth. And the LORD said unto Moses, I will do this thing also that thou hast spoken: for thou hast found grace in my sight, and I know thee by name. And he said, I beseech thee, show me thy glory. And he said, I will make all my goodness pass before thee, and I will proclaim the name of the LORD before thee; and will be gracious to whom I will be gracious, and will show mercy on whom I will show mercy. And he said, Thou canst not see my face: for there shall no man see me, and live (Exod. 33:12-20).

At this point in Moses' life, I am quite sure he would have rather seen God's face than live. He was not, however, ready for that yet.

This is the great spiritual contradiction: to long to see the face of God and be prohibited from seeing that face. In spite of the inconsistency here, the promise to Israel was that as long as they dwelt in the midst of the Shekinah glory of God, no enemy could touch them. As a nation, they delighted in the smiling face of Providence.

The Tabernacle

Following the building of the tabernacle, the Shekinah cloud came down, resting above the Holiest of Holies. This cloud ruled Israel for 40 years as they traveled in the desert, hovering over her as a visible cloud by day and a pillar of fire by night. The focus of the cloud was the tabernacle, which enjoyed the perpetual shadow of God's presence and favor.

I often wonder if the average Israeli, during that time in the wilderness, realized he or she was living under the very presence of the Lord God Jehovah. What it must have been like to get up in the morning, look out of your tent and see the presence of God hovering over the tabernacle and the Holiest of Holies, and to know Jehovah was there! Israel could not forget her God when every morning there was the visible manifestation of His presence.

Mount of Transfiguration

In the New Testament, we have a glorious example of this cloud. When Jesus and His disciples were on the Mount of Transfiguration, we see that cloud again (see Matt. 17:1-8). Those mystified disciples saw Him for the very first time as He truly was. In His transformed glory, they worshiped Him as never before. What they understood by what they saw and experienced is hard for us to comprehend. Nothing in their life up to this point prepared them for such a magnificent exhibition of the glory of Christ.

This incident on the Mount of Transfiguration gave Peter, James and John a glimpse of the glorified, transformed Christ. It is the same Christ John saw in Revelation sitting on the throne. Would I go too far astray if I said it was the same Man that Shadrach, Meshach and Abednego saw in the furnace as the fourth man, like unto the Son of God? Down through the ages, that "Fourth Man in the furnace" has revealed Himself to a variety of people. One day, all of humanity will be exposed to this Glorified One.

Peter writes about this incident in 2 Peter 1:16-21 and says they "were eyewitnesses of his majesty" (v. 16). Peter uses the word "majesty," for no other word seems to fit their experience. There is no way to define it theologically; it did not fit into any doctrinal template known to man. It is impossible to rationalize this or put it into some kind of philosophical formula. They were eyewitnesses of God's majesty and the transfigured Christ; and the way Peter addresses it in his epistle is almost in hushed awe of God's glory.

The focus on the Mount of Transfiguration, of course, was Christ. Being transfigured before them, they encountered the Mystic Shroud of the Blessed Hope. It was then that Peter, not knowing what to say, did what most people do, and said something: "Lord, it is good for us to be here: if thou wilt, let us make here three tabernacles; one for Thee, and one for Moses and one for Elias" (Matt. 17:4).

While Peter was speaking, "a bright cloud overshadowed them" (v. 5). It was the Shekinah glory of God coming down upon them. The three disciples were overwhelmed by the brilliancy of this cloud; it was unlike any cloud they had ever seen before. It was not a cloud that carried the rain, but rather it carried the majestic nature of God Himself. They found themselves enveloped in a haze of divine brilliancy and, consequently, they had no desire to leave. Who would?

From this cloud came a voice, "This is my beloved Son, in whom I am well pleased; hear ye him" (v. 5). They saw a transfigured Christ before them whose face did shine as the sun, and His raiment was white as the light. The voice, which could be none other than the voice of God Himself, declared the supremacy of this One standing before them who was well pleasing in His sight.

This experience of the transfigured Christ defied anything they had ever known up to this point; it was an experience that exhausted all human explanation. If Peter, James and John were like many people today, they would have written a book explaining in great detail and pompous authority what all this was. James never wrote about it. Peter spoke of it in 2 Peter 1 only in a hushed and holy voice. John, in Revelation, did not try to explain it; he only set forth the details as he experienced it in the fullness of Christ's majestic glory.

> And when he had spoken these things, while they beheld, he was taken up; and a cloud received him out of their sight. And while they looked steadfastly toward heaven as he went up, behold, two men stood by them in white apparel (Acts 1:9-10).

Oh, this Christ! This one sitting on the throne enshrouded with the Mystic Shroud of the glory of God's Majesty. Words fail and language is exhausted, but the redeemed heart rises up in adoration, worshiping and singing the hymn of the Lamb and the One sitting on the throne. I personally long for that songfest around the throne. Often in our church services the singing is simply performance. Oh, but one day, it will simply be in response to the manifested glory of the One sitting on the throne! It will be an offering worthy of the Lamb.

Jesus at the Center of All Prophecy

It is interesting that the very beginning of the book of Revelation starts with Christ. The very theme of the book is the Revelation of Jesus Christ. He is at the center of all prophecy. If we follow a prophetic trail that leads us away from this glorified one sitting on the throne, we can be sure we are headed for some kind of heresy. In Revelation, all lead to Christ, and all come from Christ. He is the center. He is the focus of all things. He is the one the holy elders, beasts, angels, seraphim and cherubim sing about. When the focus is not on Him, heresy develops.

The one who is sitting on the throne is the Alpha and Omega, the Beginning and the End. He is the sum total of all things that were, are or will be. Nothing can be fully understood apart from this glorious Person sitting on the throne. His presence is covered in the Mystic Shroud of the Blessed Hope.

The very keynote of all prophecy is, "This same Jesus, which is taken up from you into heaven, shall so come in like manner as ye have seen him go into heaven" (Acts 1:11). If you do not believe anything else, and if the prophetic teachers with their charts have confused you, you can at least believe this: "Behold he cometh" and "This same Jesus." This is the beginning and the end of all prophecy.

When the body of Jesus was in Joseph of Arimathea's tomb, the spirit of Jesus was preaching to the souls in prison, and His body was, for the time being, the remains in the grave. After the third day, He came back, was glorified, re-inhabited that body, rose from the grave and stood a man, alive forevermore.

The Church Fathers say, "I believe in God, the Father Almighty, and I believe in Jesus Christ, the Son who is the faithful witness and the first begotten from the dead and the Prince of the Kings of the earth." When He comes, I believe a cry will go up that will circle the earth: "Behold, He cometh!" When that cry goes up, every eye will see Him and all the families of the earth will give up their vacations, their holidays, their split-level houses, their books, their theaters, their dances and their careers—all their little earthly cares. That which occupies all their attention and focus will fail in comparison to this One who comes. Then they will have one great care. But, alas, then it will be too late, and the kings of the earth shall wail because of Him.

This same Jesus is coming, and He is coming back in like manner as He went away. He went away in a cloud as a man. He is coming back in a cloud, exactly as they saw Him go. Those who knew Him will recognize Him. All the kingdoms of the earth will recognize Him because He is a man. He is a glorified man; not a spirit, not an angel, not some creature out of the fire, but the man who walked around on this earth, who ate fish, drank the sweet waters of Galilee and said, "Mary," and to His disciples said, "Peter." This same Jesus is coming again.

The whole scope of the Bible teaches this. It is found in the books of Revelation and Daniel and Isaiah and Jeremiah; it is taught in Luke and Mark, in John, in Matthew, in Acts and in Romans and 1 and 2 Peter and 1 John. All through the Scriptures, we have this panoramic view and glorious expectation of the same Jesus coming again. This harmony of expectation is the beating heart of true Christian experience. It is simply the core of our joy and our delight as believers who long for the return of Jesus.

Isaiah tells us, "Thy dead men shall live, together with my dead body shall they arise. Awake and sing, ye that dwell in dust: for thy dew is as the dew of herbs, and the earth shall cast out the dead" (Isa. 26:19). Yes, we are going to sing.

Whenever I am at a camp meeting, I often see the American goldfinch. They have one little habit I love. As long as they are feeding, they are quiet; but stir them up and as they go, they sing. They make little motions as they fly through the air and are beautiful to look at, yellow and black. That is exactly what we are going to do. We are going to rise up and sing, "He that dwell in dust, the earth shall give forth its dead."

Lo, He Comes with Clouds Descending
John Cennick (1718–1755)

Lo! he comes with clouds descending,
Once for favored sinners slain;
Thousand thousand saints attending
Swell the triumph of his train:
Hallelujah! Hallelujah! Hallelujah!
God appears on earth to reign.

Every eye shall now behold him
Robed in dreadful majesty;
Those who set at naught and sold Him,
Pierced, and nailed Him to the tree,
Deeply wailing, deeply wailing, deeply wailing.
Shall the true Messiah see.

Every island, sea, and mountain,
Heav'n and earth, shall flee away;

All who hate Him must, confounded,
Hear the trump proclaim the day:
Come to judgment! Come to judgment!
Come to judgment!
Come to judgment! Come away!

Now redemption, long expected,
See in solemn pomp appear;
All His saints, by man rejected,
Now shall meet him in the air:
Hallelujah! Hallelujah! Hallelujah!
See the day of God appear!

The dear tokens of His passion
Still His dazzling body bears;
Cause of endless exultation
To His ransomed worshippers;
With what rapture, with what rapture,
with what rapture
Gaze we on those glorious scars!

Yea, Amen! let all adore Thee,
High on Thine eternal throne;
Savior, take the power and glory,
Claim the kingdom for Thine own;
O come quickly! O come quickly! O come quickly!
Everlasting God, come down!

8

The Authority
of the
Blessed Hope

*Thy throne above, O God, is established from eternity
past to eternity future. There is no limit to Thy authority and no
challenge whatsoever. Thy reign is filled with Thy goodness and mercy
and wisdom. Thou reignest alone and callest all things unto Thyself.
The glory of Thy wisdom is seen throughout all Thy creation.
Thou reignest in Majesty on high, and I humbly bow before
Thee in adoration and worship. Amen.*

It is difficult to move away from the throne of the Majesty in Revelation 4. John gives an accurate report of what he saw: "A throne was set in heaven, and One sat on the throne" (Rev. 4:2). Here in the heavenlies, the Majesty of the one who sat on the throne reveals Himself to John. What a revelation it was!

This is not some ordinary throne, but rather it was "a throne . . . set in heaven." The location of this throne is important. "In heaven" indicates that it is above earth and all of the authorities in earth. It is a throne to be compared with no other throne throughout the entire created universe. It is the absolute source of all authority from which all other authority derives.

It is interesting to see how John talks about the throne. He uses these phrases: "on the throne," "round about the throne," "out of the throne," "before the throne," "on the throne," and finally, in verse 10, "before the throne." The climax of this vision of the throne is when those associated with that throne and the one sitting on the throne cast their crowns before the throne, saying, "Thou art worthy, O Lord, to receive glory and honour and power; for thou hast created all things, and for thy pleasure they are and were created" (v. 11).

That which brings majesty and glory to the throne is easily seen to be the one who sat on the throne. And the harmonious heavenly reverberation surrounds the throne with continuous worship. Only this one who sits on the throne is worthy of such worship, and all of creation bows before Him in reverence and adoration.

John's vision of this throne in heaven conveys a mighty declaration to all creation. This throne is the center of all things created, and from it descends all authority, power and dominion. John attempts to describe what he sees, but his description is limited to language. Language is always clumsy, especially when trying to describe what John saw.

The Throne Declares Authority

The throne in the heavens declares God's authority, dominion and power. In John's attempt to describe the throne, one cannot help but see that from the throne comes authority. Keep in mind that the authority spoken of here is permanent authority. The one who sat on the throne did not inherit His authority from anyone, nor did He win the throne from some other. There was never a time when He did not possess all authority. His authority predates time and the creation of everything that is. And there never will be a time when His authority will be in any way diminished or even challenged.

The authority that comes from this throne is universal authority. It is not derived from anything, while all other authority is derived from this higher authority. Examples of this authority would be Lucifer's, Melchisedec's, David's, the apostles', the rulers of this world, and the list goes on and on. All of these derived their authority from some higher power. There was a time when they did not have this authority; then they had this authority given to them from a higher authority. Their authority is limited, and a time will come when it will be taken away. This authority is limited in every regard.

The declared authority from the throne in heaven is underived, permanent and unchallenged. This authority springs from God Himself by virtue of who He is and what He is and what He has done. It would be impossible to separate His authority from Himself. The kings and rulers of this world borrow their authority, but the one on the throne borrows His authority from no one. His authority comes from Himself, is infinite and does not diminish over time.

In my lifetime, I saw men like Adolf Hitler rise to a place of authority. There was a time when nobody ever heard of Adolf Hitler. Then his name was on the lips of just about every civilized person in the world. He rose in authority and power, and for a time he possessed authority. Then the time came when he died and no longer had authority, nor does his name bear any authority today. This is the borrowed authority of the creature who gets his or her authority from the Creator.

The authority of the one on the throne is absolute and universal. There is no place you can go in the entire created universe in the heavens where you could come to the end of His authority. Nothing and no one could ever bind His authority. It is absolute in every regard. David the psalmist marveled at this aspect of God. He wrote in language that only he could write:

Whither shall I go from thy spirit? or whither shall I flee from thy presence? If I ascend up into heaven, thou art there: if I make my bed in hell, behold, thou art there. If I take the wings of the morning, and dwell in the uttermost parts of the sea; Even there shall thy hand lead me, and thy right hand shall hold me. If I say, Surely the darkness shall cover me; even the night shall be light about me. Yea, the darkness hideth not from thee; but the night shineth as the day: the darkness and the light are both alike to thee (Ps. 139:7-12).

David understood that God's authority could never be eluded. He was an example of trying to get away from that authority but could not. Finally, he yielded and discovered in God's authority a great blessing. Those who challenge God's authority discover that they are no match, and they suffer the consequences of falling under the authority of God.

The Throne Declares Dominion

The one who sits on the throne exercises His authority throughout His dominion, and there is nothing outside of His dominion. Even if we could take all of the technology man has today and multiply it by 1,000, no technology will discover for us the boundary of our universe. As soon as some man believes he has found the outer limits, he discovers another galaxy he did not know existed.

This declares the sovereignty of the one who sits on the throne. From the miniscule atom to the stars in the heaven, all are subject to His sovereign will. Inescapable laws control all of creation. The stars in the heaven are subject to laws they did not create and cannot escape.

Some people in desperation will say, "Oh, that I might be as free as a bird and fly away!" The truth is, the bird does not know freedom but rather is in bondage to the laws of gravity like anyone and anything else. To contradict the laws of gravity brings a person into the conflict with that law.

No life escapes the sovereign will of this throne. All life is subject to the will established by the One who sits upon the throne. Man, for example, does not choose his own birth, his own race, his own gender. Neither does he choose the time and place of his death. All of these are subject to the sovereign will of the one who sits upon the throne. Men who can control very little shake a defiant fist at the one who sits on the throne. But that gesture in no way intimidates God.

Also subject to His sovereign will are all plans. Everything in this world contributes to the fulfillment of an eternal plan established from the throne of God. "And all that dwell upon the earth shall worship him, whose names are not written in the book of life of the Lamb slain from the foundation of the world" (Rev. 13:8). Nothing in any way contradicts the sovereign will of the throne.

Some may point out that sin appears to have defeated that purpose. Look at what is happening out in the world and the devastation sin is creating. How can that be subject to the sovereign will? As we look at the throne set in heaven, we discover a far-reaching, omniscient strategy flowing from the beginning of time. All events in every generation are in absolute harmony with the sovereign will of the throne.

When Joseph finally revealed himself to his brothers, they thought he would get even with them for all the pain and misery they had caused him. "And Joseph said unto them, Fear not: for am I in the place of God? But as for you, ye thought evil against me; but God meant it unto good, to bring to pass, as it is this day, to save much people alive" (Gen. 50:19-20).

Almighty God can turn what is meant for evil to His good. It is kind of a sour joke on the devil to realize that nothing he can do can in any wise thwart the sovereign will of God. Nothing he has ever done is outside the authority of God. The devil only utilizes a borrowed authority. The throne in the heavens declares the absolute dominion of the one who sits upon it.

The Throne Declares Power

It is conceivable that somebody can have authority to do something and yet lack the power to accomplish it. A police officer has the authority to arrest someone, but he may not have the power to bring that subject under his authority. On the other side, someone may have the power to arrest somebody, and bring them under control, but not have the authority to do it. What John sees in the heavens is a throne that not only has authority and dominion, but also has the power to accomplish the sovereign will of the throne. This power is the ability to compel obedience to a previously conceived plan. For a period of time, God will invite obedience, but there is coming a time when He will compel obedience, and all will fall into line.

He Will Accomplish It

What is God's plan? I believe God has revealed a part of His eternal plan. There are several aspects associated with it.

First, as we read the book of Revelation, I believe that God has a plan to renovate planet Earth. Sin has so demolished aspects of the planet that only God can rescue it. Part of God's plan is the renovation of the planets and the earth. Additionally, I believe that part of His plan is the reclamation of a race—humanity. Despite all the advances in philosophy, education, technology and medicine, the human race is falling apart. As soon as one disease is cured, two or three jump to take its place. There is a sickness permeating throughout the human race that demands what only the power from the throne can do.

To achieve the reclamation of humanity, two things are on God's program. One would be the glorification of the Body, that is, the Church of Jesus Christ. Even now, God is calling out people for Himself, and this Church is waiting patiently for the glorification when we all come into the presence of the one who sits on the throne.

Another plan is the restoration of a nation—Israel. Throughout history, this little nation has been taunted, teased, bruised and battered. The fact that it is still a nation is a testament of the sovereignty of God. Is there another nation upon the earth more hated today than Israel? Throughout the book of Revelation, we understand that God is going to bring this nation back to a point of glory. He will restore this nation and even sit upon the throne in Jerusalem Himself. The throne in heaven is focused down upon the throne to be established again in Israel.

This power moves out from the throne to accomplish His purposes, which are being unfolded systematically and cannot fail of accomplishment. The power flowing from the throne is uncontested, unrivaled and un-derived, and it will always accomplish the sovereign will of the throne. Coming from this throne is the grand strategy that outthinks devil and man. "And there were," John writes, "seven lamps of fire burning before the throne, which are the seven Spirits of God." Here is the absolute wisdom of God, which has devised this grand strategy.

The present question might be, Why the triumph of evil? People are full of sin and the nations are rising and falling. The vast majority of the nations today are at war. Nation seems to be against nation, and kingdom against kingdom. Evil seems to be triumphing in our world today. How can this be explained in the light of God's sovereignty?

Ah, but the one who is sitting on the throne has absolved all of this in His master plan. This master plan emanating from the throne has several characteristics of note. It has the wisdom to conceive this plan, the goodness to will it, the authority to execute it and, most importantly, the power to affect it. All of these things are necessary and are rooted in the one seated on the throne.

Although evil seems to be triumphing now, we must remember that "now" is merely a point in time. The grand strategy emulating from the throne was developed before time ever began, and time will not diminish it in any wise. John hints at this in Revelation 13, when he talks about "the lamb slain from the foundation of the world" (v. 8). Before the world ever came into existence, God had already established the plan of salvation. Sin and the evil of humanity did not catch God by surprise. All along, His sovereign will has taken into consideration man's sin. And because of the one who sits on the throne, all of the sin and all of the evil of humanity in no way intimidate the sovereign will.

Jesus declared His power to His disciples, which was the basis of their going into the world preaching the gospel: "And Jesus came and spake unto them, saying, All power is given unto me in heaven and in earth" (Matt. 28:18).

By embracing the Blessed Hope, these disciples had the authority they needed to go where Jesus directed them: into all the world. This authority did not lie in their personal experience, or in their theological understanding and expertise, or in their ability to articulate the gospel message. Nobody had better articulation than the Pharisees when it came to the Law, and nobody had less power than they did. Our authority rests in the

Blessed Hope. If our message drifts the slightest degree from the Blessed Hope, we will have forfeited all of our authority and power. It is not a message we are bringing; rather, it is the person of Jesus Christ. The authority of the Blessed Hope lies in the person of the Blessed Hope. Even so, come, Lord Jesus.

Thou Art Coming, O My Savior
Frances Ridley Havergal (1836–1879)

Thou art coming, O my Savior,
Thou art coming, O my King,
In Thy beauty all resplendent,
In Thy glory all transcendent;
Well may we rejoice and sing:
Coming! in the opening east
Herald brightness slowly swells;
Coming! O my glorious Priest,
Hear we not Thy golden bells?

Thou art coming, Thou art coming;
We shall meet Thee on Thy way,
We shall see Thee, we shall know Thee,
We shall bless Thee, we shall show Thee
All our hearts could ever say:
What an anthem that will be,
Ringing out our love to Thee,
Pouring out our rapture sweet
At Thine own all glorious feet.

Thou art coming; at Thy table
We are witnesses for this;

While remembering hearts Thou meetest
In communion clearest, sweetest,
Earnest of our coming bliss,
Showing not Thy death alone,
And Thy love exceeding great;
But Thy coming and Thy throne,
All for which we long and wait.

Thou art coming, we are waiting
With a hope that cannot fail,
Asking not the day or hour,
Resting on Thy Word of power,
Anchored safe within the veil.
Time appointed may be long,
But the vision must be sure;
Certainty shall make us strong,
Joyful patience can endure.

O the joy to see Thee reigning,
Thee, my own beloved Lord!
Every tongue Thy Name confessing,
Worship, honor, glory, blessing
Brought to Thee with glad accord;
Thee, my Master and my Friend,
Vindicated and enthroned;
Unto earth's remotest end
Glorified, adored, and owned!

Cyril Carlin
10 Wilton Cres
Dartmouth NS B2V 2S9

9

THE TRUE HOPE
OF THE
BLESSED HOPE

Thou, O God, hast urged me to seek Thy face; and Thy face,
O God, have I sought with all my heart. All around me is trouble
and wickedness and failure. The only remedy is in Thee.
I come before Thee with great hope and encouragement. I look
to the world and am greatly disappointed, but when I gaze upon
Thy face, I find true rest for my soul. Only in Thee is there
any hope for all humanity. Amen.

When the door opened in heaven, it revealed the throne and the one seated on the throne. It also showed a rainbow encircling the throne, and round about the throne were the 24 elders. Before the throne were the four living creatures. There was lightning and thunder, and in the midst of it all was worship from all creation as the living creatures, which represent all of the unfallen creation, and the elders, representative of all the redeemed creation, joined to worship the Lord. Although the scene does not change, John also saw and recorded that mighty deeds are done here.

John was still looking through that open door at the throne and all its wonders when he also saw the mighty deeds done before the throne—the all-embracing, breathtaking, cosmic deeds that are mighty in their extent and power.

John looked through this open door into heaven. And later he wrote, "And I saw, in the right hand of him that sat on the throne a book written within and on the backside, sealed with seven seals" (Rev. 5:1). This book was so full that it was written on the inside and the backside so that it was twice as big a book as it would have been otherwise.

The Title Deed to the World

Many who have tried to explain this book have stumbled, causing others to stumble. This is the result of cold textualism—trying to interpret Scripture, especially prophetic Scripture, from a merely intellectual viewpoint. "This book was written in tears," somebody said, "and it can only be understood in tears." That probably comes as close as anything I can think of to say about the scene. In the context of what John was seeing, I have concluded that this book is the title deed to the world. At this point, the Church has been taken up and is with the Lord.

Claims to the Title Deed

We see the elders, who represent all the redeemed; and the creatures, who represent all the unfallen. And now we are going to settle forever a big question: Who owns the world? That question must be answered because there was a dark and dreadful day when God's right to the world was challenged, and the ownership of the world was questioned. Satan and his hosts claimed the world and have been fighting for it ever since. Satan's words to Christ in the wilderness indicated that he thought he had a claim on the title deed to the world: "Again, the devil taketh him up into an exceeding high mountain, and sheweth him all the kingdoms of the world, and the glory of them; And saith unto him, All these things will I give thee, if thou wilt fall down and worship me" (Matt. 4:8-9).

The big question behind the scene is, who really owns the earth? The whole chronicling of history has tried to answer this one basic question. Many contenders for this position have caused havoc throughout the centuries.

Some have said that the great thinkers of the world own the earth. These are the philosophers, the brains—the men who habitually inhabit altitudes of philosophical thought that most people never get to. Some only get to this for just a few minutes, and then they desert it for the rest of their lives. They get a little taste of the highlands, and then say, "I'll never read that book again." There have been great philosophers, great thinkers and great inventors who have, for a period of time, thought they owned the world.

The book of Ecclesiastes is a book of a great thinker who only got unhappier as he went along. He said, "For in much wisdom is much grief: and he that increaseth knowledge increaseth sorrow" (Eccles. 1:18). Many people, sad to say, have never experienced this kind of sorrow personally.

Some would point to the worker and say it is the man who toils who owns the world. "Workers of the world, arise; you've nothing to lose but your chains," they said in the early 1900s. Therefore, the proletariat was said to own the world.

Others believe that the world belongs to the man who can take it. Men such as Hitler had the mistaken idea that the world belonged to the person who could take it, namely himself. He tried, and history has recorded it for us. When one Hitler succumbs to the inevitable, another one seems to rise up and take his place. In this regard, history seems to repeat itself *ad nauseam.*

Of course, we have the statesmen who have laid claim to ownership of the world. Every nation has had its great statesman, because they could not be a nation without a statesman to establish it. Whether it was the largest or the smallest nation, somebody had to be known as the father of his country.

Closely aligned with the statesmen are the politicians who, in order to prove they own the world, start wars to conquer parts of the world. No war would be possible apart from the back-room dealings of politicians down through the ages. If only we, the common people, knew what went on behind closed doors that led to some war, we would be shocked.

Then we come to the scientist. I believe it is a cynical and ominous thing that the scientists have become the high priests of the great god science in these last days. Learned men and scientists labor under the misunderstanding that they could own the world. Scientists are able to heal one disease while other scientists who are equally reputable and honorable men invent ways to destroy the greatest number of men in the quickest time. I could continue this by citing the painters, the poets, the dreamers and artists of the world. All, in his or her own right, has laid claim to the ownership of the world.

It has always seemed rather silly to me that the man with the biggest fist has the right to anything. There sits a car in a parking lot. Two men walk up, a little man and a big one, and someone says, "Who owns this car?" The little man says, "I own it." The big man says, "No, I own it." Therefore, they decide to find out who owns it by fighting, and the fellow with the biggest fist says, "It's mine." They have not proved who owned the car, only who had the biggest fists.

That seems to be the way with nations too. When they start a war, they do not prove anything. All they prove is who can fight the most and the best, and last the longest.

The Indisputable Owner of the Title Deed

When the tentacles of hell are shaken loose from the world and the world is given back to the one who owns it, there will be no deception. Nobody will pull any tricks, and nobody will do any arguing. There will not be any need for arguing. Nobody will do any bullying, and nobody will do any lying, because they are in the face of God, who knows a lie when He hears it, and no force will be needed. Somebody is going to determine who owns this world after all. The reign of Christ is the divine imperative.

What John points out here in Revelation 5 is that the one to rule the world is the one who is *worthy* to rule the world. John looked around for someone who could establish claim to it and say, "This is mine, and I have a right to it. I have a right to shake the tentacles of hell loose from it, because it doesn't belong to them." No living creature, no beast with four faces, no archangel with a great wingspread, no cherubim, no seraphim, no creature other than human had any right to this earth.

By right, the earth belongs to humanity, because we are made in the image of God, and this is our playground, our back-yard, our front yard, our meadow. The world is the place where we play and work and live and die, but it has been taken from us. The one to rule had to have the right relationship. The one who is worthy to rule had to be first of the seed of Abraham. There had to be somebody with character good enough to want to do it and wise enough to know how to do it and holy and pure and powerful enough to do it. No one could qualify, and they searched everywhere.

As the book is brought into focus, only the owner could open it: "And I saw," John says, "a strong angel proclaiming with a loud voice, Who is worthy to open the book, and to loose the seals thereof?" (Rev. 5:2). What a search that must have been!

But no man in earth and no man under the earth could be found that was worthy. John saw this, and it was too much for him. "I wept much" (v. 4), John wrote. Being a tender man, John wept much because no man was found worthy or able to open and read the book. To do this, one had to have certain qualifications. He had to have authority.

Christ's Authority Revealed to the Heart in Tune with His

John was a man who carried the grief of the human race in his heart. Because God carried the grief of the human race in His heart, He sent and signified it by the angel unto His servant John. God always tells the man who cares, and He does not tell the man who does not care. This is why prophetic teaching went astray more than a generation back. Too many had no concern. They were simply curious and studied and taught from other motives than a genuine concern.

God always blesses the man with tears in his eyes, and He always gives information to the man with concern in his heart. If you have a concern in your heart and go before God on your knees, you will get more information that matters than can be taught in seminaries. I believe in education, but I say that we will get more information with a broken heart. God will reveal things to a man with a broken heart, but He will not reveal things unless the man's heart is broken. To try to learn divine things and peer into divine mysteries and penetrate the veil without having tears in our eyes and sorrow in our hearts is vanity and futility a hundred times multiplied.

John wrote, "And I wept much, because no man was found worthy to open and to read the book, neither to look thereon" (v. 4). That was not the end of the story. In the midst of John's weeping, one of the elders stepped forward and said, "Weep not, behold, the Lion of the tribe of Judah, the Root of David, hath prevailed to open the book, and to loose the seven seals thereof" (v. 5). A man was found. A man prevailed and was worthy to claim the title deed of the world.

Our hope is that there is one coming again, and He is going to take the book and break the seals and take over the world. He will shake Satan loose from the world that he does not rightfully own and give it into the hands that were once crucified for humanity.

We can see the distress of nations. There are a hundred remedies offered, but not one works. Christians have the only true hope. It is the message concerning the one who is worthy—the Lord Jesus Christ.

Worthy Is the Lamb
Johnson Oatman, Jr. (1856–1922)

"Worthy is the Lamb," the hosts of Heaven sing,
As before the throne they make His praises ring;
"Worthy is the Lamb the book to open wide,
Worthy is the Lamb who once was crucified."

Worthy is the Lamb, who shed His precious blood
To restore a world to happiness and God;
When no eye could pity and no arm could save,
Jesus for our ransom, Himself freely gave.

Worthy is the Lamb, the bleeding sacrifice
Who for Adam's race paid such a fearful price;

Worthy is the Lamb, the Paschal Lamb of God,
For the world received Redemption thro' His blood.

"Worthy is the Lamb," let men and angels sing,
"Worthy is the Lamb," let hallelujahs ring;
And when life is past, upon the golden shore,
"Worthy is the Lamb," we'll shout forevermore.

Oh, this bleeding Lamb, oh, this bleeding Lamb,
Oh, this dying Lamb, He was found worthy;
Oh, this bleeding Lamb, oh, this bleeding Lamb,
Oh, this dying Lamb, He was found worthy.

10

THE NATURE BEHIND THE BLESSED HOPE

*O God, my voice joins the worship crescendo around
the throne as the Lamb is proclaimed worthy. I weep no more, for
Thou hast conquered. Thou art worthy, O Lamb, to receive glory and
honor and praise, for Thou hast conquered and goeth forth to conquer.
I join the four and twenty elders as they fall down and worship You,
who liveth forever and ever. Amen.*

Rooted in the Old Testament is the lion, the symbol of Judah, one of the 12 tribes of Israel and the ruling tribe in Israel. In courage and strength, might, dominion and rulership, all belonged to Judah. And out of Judah came the kings, David and Solomon, culminating in the King of kings and Lord of lords, Jesus Christ. "The scepter shall not depart from Judah," said the Lord, "nor a lawgiver from between his feet, until Shiloh come; and unto him shall the gathering of the people be" (Gen. 49:10).

Here in Revelation 5, we see Jesus Christ as the Lion of the tribe of Judah. See that lion there, tawny gold in the moonlight. This great untamed lion with its head held high and its eyes sweeping the plain and then lowering its head and roaring its challenge to the world. All the little creatures everywhere are frightened; some of them flee in a panic, some cower and some freeze among the leaves, hoping the lion will pass them by. This mighty Lion of the tribe of Judah symbolizes Christ Jesus the

Lord; and He has conquered. This is the New Testament shout of triumph that He has prevailed to open the book.

When John the Revelator heard them say, "Behold, the lion of the tribe of Judah, the root of David, had prevailed to open the book, and to loose the seven seals thereof," he no doubt expected to see a great tawny lion with His head held high and His long angry tail switching in the light. But when he turned about, expecting to see the Lion, John says, "And I beheld, and, lo, in the midst of the throne and of the four beasts, and in the midst of the elders, stood a Lamb as it had been slain, having seven horns and seven eyes, which are the seven Spirits of God sent forth into all the earth" (Rev. 5:6).

Because a lion conquers by tooth and claw, John turned in fear, anticipating seeing the Lion, but saw instead the Lamb. He turned to see that the Lion/Lamb had prevailed to take the book—the title deed to the world—out of the hand of the great God Almighty.

God's Ways Baffle All Understanding

God's ways and man's ways are not identical. On earth, the lion is stronger than the lamb; but in the kingdom of God and before the face of God, the Lamb is stronger than the Lion. And here was one who was both.

When John the Baptist saw Jesus, he said, "Behold the Lamb of God . . ." (John 1:29). When John the Revelator saw Jesus, he saw Him as a Lamb. But He is both Lion and Lamb. Unless we know this, we are not Christians in the right sense of the word and are not well-taught Christians, as we ought to be.

Christians used to talk about Jesus as the Lion, and they made a great deal over Him being Conqueror and Victor. But we have come to think of Him only as the Lamb. In our way of thinking, either He is the Lamb or He is the Lion, but He cannot be both. From the kingdom of heaven, He is both Lion and Lamb. Keep in mind that what the Lion will do is always a result of what the Lamb did.

In this regard, the redemption of the world is completely out of the hands of man. Thankfully, redemption was done the way God does things, not the way man does them. If man had his way, the plan of redemption would be an endless and bloody conflict. In reality, salvation was bought not by Jesus' fists, but by His nail-pierced hands; not by muscle but by love; not by vengeance but by forgiveness; not by force but by sacrifice. Jesus Christ our Lord surrendered in order that He might win; He destroyed His enemies by dying for them and conquered death by allowing death to conquer Him.

This is not the way man does it. We see that starting with Cain and Abel (see Gen. 4), man has his way by physical dominance. The man who can hit the hardest takes the prize and gets the trophy. That is the way of man. But God says, "I won't put Myself in the hands of men." The whole work of redemption has to be done the way things are done in heaven. There are two kingdoms, the kingdom of heaven and the kingdom of man. In man's kingdom, it is knuckles and muscles that count, along with vengeance and hate. In heaven, it is love and sacrifice. Giving out of love is more powerful than all the armies of the world.

When the disciples asked Jesus to teach them how to pray, He included in that prayer this whole idea of kingdom authority. "And he said unto them, When ye pray, say, Our Father which art in heaven, Hallowed be thy name. Thy kingdom come. Thy will be done, as in heaven, so in earth" (Luke 11:2). The essence of that prayer is to bring the kingdom of heaven to bear upon the affairs of earth. The beginning of that is in man's salvation. That salvation has no roots in earth, but rather in the kingdom of heaven.

The truth is now known. In Revelation 5, we are not dealing only with Israel; we are not dealing only with the Church; we are not dealing only with the nations of the world; but rather, we are dealing with the entire created universe. The whole universe is being searched through, and the whole universe is waiting to see who is the one, and how it could be that this one is capable of and worthy of the place of rulership over the world.

The wondering universe learns that sin has come to the earth and turned it upside down and confounded humanity to such a point that man always thinks upside down. You can be perfectly sure about one thing: An unconverted man thinking about religion always thinks wrong. Man is always upside down, and a Christian has to be always correcting his own heart and translating what he hears into the language of heaven so that he will not be carried away by the world. Man has learned the way of the Lion, and it is the way of the Lion that prevails.

The history of the world is humanity dripping with blood, like the midnight path of the lion. We are what we are and we have what we have because somebody with a big fist and tough muscles and a long sword and a heavy hammer or big cannon was able to take it and hold it for us. The question of justice and righteousness scarcely comes up at all. The mighty take over and rule the weaker. Men conquer by spilling the blood of their enemies.

The Lamb Prevails

How odd of God that He should do this wondrous thing, that He should run contrary to the ways of man. Man has learned the ways of the lion, the power of guns, what prisons will do, how to make armies march, and how to throw bombs. He has learned what force will do and how selfish men get their own way in the world. Then along comes the great God Almighty and does a wonderful thing.

Christ conquered by shedding His own blood. It was the first time in the history of the world it was ever thought of, and it has never been thought of since. When man conquers, he always conquers by spilling the blood of others, certainly not his own. Christ conquered by spilling His own blood. There was the Lamb who became the Lion by shedding His own blood, giving Himself up in death for humanity.

Now He stands in the midst of the throne, and God has a message to the entire universe. He has a message to the world where mighty men beat their chests, where the lion is king and the way to the throne is always stained with blood. God declares, "I do things the way I do things, and I don't count upon human muscle and a human fist and human sinew. I do not count upon the beauty of the women, the strength of men or the brilliance or intelligence of anybody. I do it my way."

"For my thoughts are not your thoughts, neither are your ways my ways, saith the LORD. For as the heavens are higher than the earth, so are my ways higher than your ways, and my thoughts than your thoughts" (Isa. 55:8-9). So Jesus Christ came down and conquered the world by dying as a Lamb, and made Himself worthy to be the Lion, to rule the world by dying as a Lamb for the sins of the world.

The Lamb conquers, but the day is coming when the Lion is going to go out and take over the world. It starts in Revelation 6, when the first seals are opened and the mighty power begins to operate, and the Lord Jesus Christ cleanses the world and establishes His reign. However, it is only because He was the Lamb that He could do it. If He had not been willing to be the Lamb, the Lion would never have accomplished it.

The devil, thinking that Jesus had adopted the philosophy of Adam, took Him up to a high mountain and said, "See all the kingdoms of the world? They are all mine and I can do with them what I will. I'll give them to you, if you get down on your knees and worship me" (see Matt. 4:8-10). He thought Jesus was going to surrender. He was going to go out and conquer the world and take over the kingdoms of the world, or ride into Jerusalem with a crown on His head and establish Himself on a royal throne and wield the scepter over the kingdoms of the world. Jesus quoted a verse of Scripture and sent the devil packing. Jesus calmly went out, with His face set like flint, to die like a Lamb.

Now we see Him before the throne, standing in the midst of the throne, surrounded by the beasts and the elders, carrying the insignia of universal authority, not on the mane of a Lion, but on the head of the Lamb. The horns represent the power, and the eyes of the sevenfold Spirit represent all knowledge and all wisdom. He is ready to take over.

This is why following Christ is both easy and hard. It is hard because the ways of God and the ways of man are not equal. Man has his philosophies, techniques and methodologies and is directly opposed to the ways of God. It is easy because Jesus Christ has prevailed and is worthy to rule from the throne. If we serve God in man's way, we will make a mess of it, which is the condition of many Christians today. We are trying to serve God in man's way instead of serving God in God's way. We serve God in the way of the Lion instead of in the way of the Lamb.

The one who takes the book is worthy to rule and conquer because He died; and He could win because He surrendered. He could have dominion because He yielded dominion. He came and took the book out of the right hand of Him that sat upon the throne. Everybody recognized what that meant. Here is the one that has prevailed. They searched heaven and earth and hell, but found nobody; but right here before the throne, in plain sight, is the One who prevailed and took the book.

O For a Thousand Tongues to Sing
Charles Wesley (1707–1788)

O for a thousand tongues to sing
My great Redeemer's praise,
The glories of my God and King,
The triumphs of His grace!

My gracious Master and my God,
Assist me to proclaim,
To spread through all the earth abroad,
The honors of Thy name.

Jesus! The name that charms our fears,
That bids our sorrows cease;
'Tis music in the sinner's ears;
'Tis life, and health, and peace.

He breaks the power of canceled sin;
He sets the prisoner free.
His blood can make the foulest clean;
His blood availed for me.

He speaks, and, listening to His voice,
New life the dead receive,

The mournful, broken hearts rejoice,
The humble poor believe.

Hear Him, ye deaf; His praise, ye dumb,
Your loosened tongues employ;
Ye blind, behold your Savior come,
And leap, ye lame, for joy.

In Christ your Head, you then shall know,
Shall feel your sins forgiven;
Anticipate your heaven below,
And own that love is heaven.

Glory to God and praise and love
Be ever, ever giv'n
By saints below and saints above
The church in earth and heav'n.

11

THE SOUND OF THE BLESSED HOPE

O heavenly Father, our hearts are filled with fear and anxiety as we hear the sound of the world around us. Oh, God, lift up our hearts that we might hear the sound of the Blessed Hope that brings to our hearts gladness and joy, that leads us into an ecstatic phase of worship, as we know that our redemption draweth nigh. Amen.

In Revelation 5, we saw the excitement of the heavenly spheres. We saw the intense interest, eager expectation, fear, hope, disclosure, general assembly and the ecstatic worship. The Lion, who became a Lamb, stepped forward to receive the title deed to the world.

Revelation 5 dealt with the ownership of the world. If you know anything about political or economic history, or the history of various social philosophies, you know that they have had various opinions on this. The world belongs to this class or that class; but God is revealing now, in Revelation 6, that the world belongs to the one who is worthy and can prove He is worthy by opening the seals.

They could not find anybody in heaven, on earth or in hell. They searched everywhere and, at last, the Lamb rose. The Lion of the tribe of Judah ascended, and those around the throne burst into glorious acclamation and ecstatic worship and said, "Worthy is the Lamb that was slain to receive power, and riches, and wisdom, and strength, and honour, and glory, and blessing" (Rev. 5:12).

The Lamb now comes forward, takes the book and opens one of the seals. The mighty creature in the midst of the throne, full of eyes and with a voice like thunder says, "Come and see" (Rev. 6:1). And John saw the waiting four horses. The hour had come for them to gallop forth. These four horses are chomping at the bit, and the four horsemen are waiting to ride forth. But they had to wait for the right time.

Generation after generation of Christians have written about and believed that the Lord was going to come at a specific time; when He did not come, they were discouraged, and some turned away from the faith and said, "He didn't come, and He won't come." Even in Peter's day, this had to be addressed: "And saying, Where is the promise of his coming? for since the fathers fell asleep, all things continue as they were from the beginning of the creation" (2 Pet. 3:4).

Man does not have the patience or the power to wait, but God does. He has all of eternity to accomplish His purposes. Therefore, all of creation waits upon the clue from the Creator.

The Four Horsemen

So, who are these horsemen? What is their purpose? How do they fit into the Blessed Hope? Let's examine each in turn.

The Rider on the White Horse

Some say that the rider of the white horse in Revelation 6:2 is Jesus Christ. I can understand how at first this might seem plausible; but in the context, I cannot see how that can be. This white horse is carrying the Antichrist, who comes conquering by duplicity. This is the dynamic of his influence. When the Antichrist wants to put something across, he says, "You've got to love everybody." While you are busy loving everybody, they steal your back teeth. While you are busy loving everybody, they take over and run the world. Whenever anybody touts the need for "coexistence," look out; they are trying to put you to sleep so they can take over something.

Liberals and unbelievers say, "Unity, brotherhood and love to all: the Man of love came to the world at Christmastime amid jingle bells and jolliness and holiday festivities. Let's all love everybody." While you are busy loving everybody, they are busy teaching our young people things like Moses did not write the Pentateuch; God did not create the heaven or the earth; there was no Adam or Eve; there was no Fall of man; Moses did not lead Israel across the Red Sea; the story of Jonah and the whale is a myth; Christ never rose from the dead; He was not born of the virgin Mary, but was the son of some German soldier. You might say this sounds blasphemous. Well, it is blasphemous, and men teach it from the pulpit in the name of "love everybody and greet each other with a holy kiss."

This duplicity is the hallmark of the Antichrist. By using the latest technique, psychological conditioning, advertising, slick publicity build-up, economic prosperity, financial security, social acceptance and promise of peace, the Antichrist is getting a death grip on the world.

The Rider on the Red Horse

Right after this false peace and prosperity, and brotherhood and unity, and one religion and security, and tolerance and all the rest, comes the Red Horse in Revelation 6:3-4, which represents war. The Antichrist is not able to keep men from warring; in fact, his plan is just the opposite. So, following hard upon the peace of the White Horse comes war.

When Mussolini came to power, he brought Italy out of a tailspin economy; everybody had money in their pockets. Then he started his wars. When Hitler came to power, the same thing happened; and so it goes as history repeats itself. Always it has been that you can only have prosperity by war and never any other way. This is the ploy of the coming Antichrist.

The world is living on a war basis, and it is the billions of dollars we are spending around the world for war and to keep our soldiers and sailors and airmen going that gives us any economic prosperity we have now. The Antichrist will find out how to use it for his purposes. Whoever controls the economy will control the world.

The Rider on the Black Horse

Following immediately upon the Red Horse, which is war, comes the Black Horse in Revelation 6:5-6, representing famine. Everybody knows how famine follows war. War creates a dislocation of things with long seasons in which farmers are not farming. The men who would raise cattle are not raising them, and the people who produce food cannot produce it, and the factories are shut down or running at a slow pace. Soon the dislocated masses throughout the world begin to starve, and we have famine. War is the main cause of famine.

The Pale Horse

The fourth horse in Revelation 6:7-8 is called death. The horrible part is that hell rides along behind war, causing bacteriological warfare and natural warfare along with pestilence and famine. I cannot see any valid reason for our saying, "Cheer up, world. We're all going to be fine for all that and all that." Not all will be well while I hear the chomping of those horses and see upon their backs those symbolic creatures right now.

Today the world holds its breath. The chant of the states-man is for a just and lasting peace and prosperity and preserva-tion of the nations and all the rest. "We are, after all," boasts the statesman, "a peace-loving nation." Certainly, no sane man wants war for itself; however, men want things that create war. Nobody wants to go to hell, but we want to live in a way that will send us there finally. Nobody wants to go to jail, but men want to do things that finally put them in jail. There is not a nation in the world that wants war. However, they do things that eventually lead to war.

The Danger of the Times

Here the Four Horses are chomping at their bits, waiting, and the world knows it not. Only those whose eyes, ears and hearts God has touched can know the danger of the times. While these horsemen wait, men are violating the holy laws of God. The scientists pry into the secrets of God while at the same time ignoring or denying the God of the secrets. The politi-cians are lusting for power and eventually create the atmo-sphere for war.

"Be wise now therefore, O ye kings: be instructed, ye judges of the earth" (Ps. 2:10). The common people do not know what the scientists and politicians have done. So the common people settle it by seeking pleasure, pampered opulence, comfort, fun and entertainment for themselves. The common person has so much that they do not know what to do with it and throw out enough in garbage each week to feed thousands of families in other parts of the world. While the rest of the world is falling apart, we are spending billions on fun.

Whether you agree with every detail I've said is not that important. But you must agree with the main points. Jesus warned that nation will rise against nation, and there will be wars everywhere throughout the world, and evil men will get worse and worse until the end, and love will wax cold. The Church will backslide and become perilous. You cannot deny that, and there is not any other interpretation for that. We may have different opinions on the details and symbols; but on the main truth here, you cannot get around it. Into the world, soon there will ride forth the White Horse, the Black Horse, the Red Horse and the Pale Horse. Then they will know in heaven, earth and hell that this world belongs, not to men, but to Jesus Christ, the man who, with His blood, purchased the earth back to Himself.

If you can imagine that, you cannot continue to live at peace and pampered opulence and without even remembering to pray for the poor, dying world. I cannot see how you could be ready for the hour when our Lord shall call His people home. I think we ought to spend time in prayer, waiting before God, seeking Him. I think we ought to drop off some things we are doing that are perfectly normal and all right, and though not harmful, they are keeping us from prayer. We ought to drop them off in order that we might spend more time kneeling before our God.

I pray that God will help us that we will not be caught here. Pray that you might be worthy to escape these things and stand before the Son of Man. I pray for myself. I want to be a more serious-minded Christian than I have ever been in my whole life. I, for my part, want to be more detached from this world than I have ever been in my life. I want to be more ready for heaven than ever before. I want to know the voice of the enemy, whether it comes from religion or politics or philosophy. I want to know when I am hearing the soft, soothing voice of the Antichrist, preparing me psychologically for a takeover. I want to know it, and I would rather stand and have everybody my enemy than go along with the crowd to destruction.

There's a passage in the book of Amos that has always bothered me:

> Woe to them that are at ease in Zion, and trust in the mountain of Samaria, which are named chief of the nations, to whom the house of Israel came! Pass ye unto Calneh, and see; and from thence go ye to Hamath the great: then go down to Gath of the Philistines: be they better than these kingdoms? or their border greater than your border? Ye that put far away the evil day, and cause the seat of violence to come near; That lie upon beds of ivory, and stretch themselves upon their couches, and eat the lambs out of the flock, and the calves out of the midst of the stall; That chant to the sound of the viol, and invent to themselves instruments of musick, like David; That drink wine in bowls, and anoint themselves with the chief ointments: but they are not grieved for the affliction of Joseph. Therefore now shall they go captive with the first that go captive, and the banquet of them that stretched themselves shall be removed (Amos 6:1-7).

With the sound of the Blessed Hope about to burst upon us, we should be excited about the prospect. All through history, men have claimed ownership of the world and forced their claim on humanity. However, that time is fast running out. The sounds of the Blessed Hope are rustling in the top of the mulberry trees. Surely, it cannot be long. Surely, the time of Jesus' return is nigh. "Even so, come, Lord Jesus" (Rev. 22:20).

When Thy Mortal Life Is Fled
Samuel Francis Smith (1808–1895)

When thy mortal life is fled,
When the death-shades o'er thee spread,
When is finished thy career,
Sinner, where wilt thou appear?

When the world has passed away,
When draws near the judgment-day,
When the awful trump shall sound,
Say, oh, where wilt thou be found?

When the Judge descends in light,
Clothed in majesty and might,
When the wicked quail with fear,
Where, oh, where wilt thou appear?

What shall soothe thy bursting heart,
When the saints and thou must part,
When the good with joy are crowned,
Sinner, where wilt thou be found?

While the Holy Ghost is nigh,
Quickly to the Saviour fly:
Then shall peace thy spirit cheer:
Then in heaven shalt thou appear.

12

THE TRIUMPH OF THE BLESSED HOPE

*O God and Father of our Lord and Savior Jesus Christ, we bow
before Thee in holy expectation of Thy gracious acceptance. The world
has been harsh and unbelieving and has brutally martyred
Thy saints. Yet, the cries of these dear ones under the altar have come
unto Thine ears. Thou wilt soon avenge the blood of those saints and
bring glory to Thy blessed name. Amen.*

The opening of the first four seals will bring much devastation to the world. Apart from the Lion of the tribe of Judah, who only is worthy to open the book, the title deed of the world, all would certainly be lost.

In the opening of the fifth seal, in Revelation 6, John sees an altar. Is this altar on earth or in heaven? Some say it is on earth because the scene is earthly. Let me call your attention to something in the book of Revelation. The entire book shifts continually, as though God were playing a tremendously powerful spotlight. First on heaven and then on earth and then back on heaven and then back to earth again, and it continues to shift between these two places so much that it takes a great deal of careful reading and exegesis to know whether a thing is on earth or in heaven.

This altar, I would take to be in the heavens above. It is unlike any altar we have here on earth. "I saw under the altar,"

John testifies, "the souls of them that were slain for the word of God, and for the testimony which they held" (Rev. 6:9). These souls are waiting under the altar and, obviously, their patience is running low, for they cry, "How long, O Lord, holy and true dost thou not judge and avenge our blood on them that dwell on the earth?" (v. 10). Certainly, we can understand the cries of these who were slain. God comforts and assures them that there are more to be added to their numbers. God is in control, and all things are in His holy hands.

The Prayers of the Martyrs

Here are the souls of the martyrs, from holy Steven to the latest one of which we will never know until we get there ourselves. My question is, why have they not been heard from before? Why have these martyred people not been heard of before this point in history? The reason is very simple: the book had not been opened. Nobody was worthy to open the book until the Lion of the tribe of Judah came along and was found worthy to open the book. Until the book was open, the seals were closed.

While we are alive, God's timing is not always known and, apparently, not after death either, because these persons were dead. It is a solemn thought that the blood of every martyred, wronged or murdered saint cries from the ground, and their souls cry from under the altar. History is all mixed up, but the omission God knows, and He knows where everybody is. He knows where all the bones and dust of the saints are. The omniscient God knows all.

What are these souls under the altar praying? And when will these prayers be fulfilled? When Jesus was with His disciples, they asked Him to teach them how to pray. From that, we have what we refer to as the Lord's Prayer:

And he said unto them, When ye pray, say, Our Father
which art in heaven, Hallowed be thy name. Thy kingdom come. Thy will be done, as in heaven, so in earth
(Luke 11:2).

I would not hesitate to say that on any given Sunday, in
any church across our country, the average Christian reciting
the Lord's Prayer has no idea what that prayer means. If, per-
chance, a person would know what he or she was praying, he
or she would be shocked and cease praying immediately. The
problem with today's Christian Church is seen right here in
the Lord's Prayer. The focus of the prayer is in the phrase, "Thy
kingdom come. Thy will be done, as in heaven, so in earth."
Few Christians really want God's kingdom to come. Fewer still
want God's will to be done in earth as it is in heaven. If that
were the case, the average Christian's life would have to be rad-
ically and dramatically altered.

What would this world be like if God's will were done here
on earth as it is in heaven? What would life be like if God's will
were never challenged but submitted to reverently and obedi-
ently? For this, the saints are praying. This is what the Christian Church is focused on as the primary aspect of their prayer
life and the expectation of the soon return of Jesus Christ. We
want Christ to return to this earth so that God's will in
heaven is accomplished here on earth. That will only happen
when Jesus Christ returns. White robes are given to the saints
under the altar, and they are assured that their cries do not
go unheeded. At God's appointed time, their prayer will be
gloriously answered.

A ransomed man is comprised of four states. There is a
time when he is lost on earth. He is without hope, without
God in this world, whose sins are piled on him; he has the

judgment of death on him, and he is lost. Then he passes out of that door into the kingdom of God and is saved on earth. He walks around for a while saved on earth. Then when that man dies, he waits in heaven. When the Lord returns, he is glorified in heaven. These are the four states of a man: lost on earth, saved on earth, waiting in heaven, and then glorified.

The Lord is not as concerned about the body as people seem to be. Nothing is mentioned here about the body, but God is going to resurrect the bodies of the saints and those who are not saints. Everybody is going to be given his or her body again.

The Fatal Mistake of Putting Trust in Men

We read about the opening of the sixth seal in Revelation 6:12. This is something we can expect, but when, I do not know. Many have tried to predict and always get in trouble when they do, because the Lord told us not to predict. But you may be sure that we are going to see a heavenly phenomenon.

The sun and moon have not yet been affected; neither the stars in their courses; but they will be. God is going to take things out of human hands. We have the contrast from this picture versus the missiles and satellites men have developed through the years. The greatest of man's technology is nothing compared to the awesomeness of Almighty God. Yet it is a fatal mistake to put our trust in men. Although we will find man offering the solution to the world's problem, for the most part, man does not understand what that problem is. For many, it is an opportunity simply to take a slice of glory.

Today, the kings of the earth are the politicians. Regardless of political party, the world is too big for any man to carry around on his shoulders. Yet, most politicians talk as if they are doing it, and I have always thought that to be rather amazing.

When the stars begin to fall, and the glory begins to shine, and the souls of the martyrs begin to plead and God begins to speak, then the politicians are going to stop making speeches and cry for the rocks and the mountains to fall on them (see Rev. 6:15-17).

We also have the great men, the heavy thinkers, who sit around thinking up great ideas and putting them to work until those ideas blow up in their faces. They will cry for the rocks and the mountains to fall on them as well.

Then there are the rich men, the lords of finance. They believe their money can solve all problems. There may be a few problems money can solve, but for the most part, the problems of the world do not have a price tag. Those who look to solve the problems through finance are going to discover what real poverty is all about.

The chief captains are the military. Some believe that every problem can be solved by military action; and so, every nation under God's heaven has invested heavily in military operations. If there is a problem somewhere in the world, they immediately jump up and boast that they can solve that problem through military action. For every problem the military can solve, it creates several more problems.

Then there are the bondmen, representing, of course, the slave world. This slavery could be many things. Maybe the reference here is to those who are slaves to a political ideology.

The last category is the free men, which could be a reference to the Western world and democracy. They believe they have the answer to solve all of the problems in the world. They boast of their freedom, and yet in the midst of their freedom is a bondage that effectively binds.

All of these offer a solution to the problems of the world, but they all fail in the end. Yes, there are periods of success and prosperity, or whatever you want to call it, but it is the end result that really matters.

Today, the ideological curtains have disappeared, and there are no bamboo curtains or iron curtains. The rich men and the great men and the sea captains and kings and freemen and the bondmen all alike cry out and say, "Fall on us, and hide us from the face of him that sitteth on the throne, and from the wrath of the Lamb" (v. 16). They pray at last, but alas, it is too late. When everything was going their way, they used the name of God as a curse word. Now, when things have turned so violently against them, they are calling out for this God to save them from the wrath of the Lamb.

There is no place for the name of Jesus Christ in the United Nations. They have a place for all religions, but no place dedicated to Jesus, the Lamb that taketh away the sins of the world. There will come a day when the United Nations, wherever it is at that time, will forget who they are and cry to the heavens above and call on a God they did not believe in and neglected, and they will say, "Fall on us, and hide us from the face of him that sitteth on the throne, and from the wrath of the Lamb: For the great day of his wrath is come."

Who Will Be Able to Stand?

When the Lamb breaks the sixth seal, John writes, "For the great day of his wrath is come; and who shall be able to stand?" (Rev. 6:17). Boast as they will, the great of this world will not be able to stand against the wrath of the Lamb.

The reason these great men are in such terror is that they love their sin. Who then shall be able to stand? Only those who have confessed their sin and quit it. Those who have given up their trinkets; those who have quit loving the world; those who have given up the hope that anything down here is permanent; and those who hate their sin as God hates it; they will stand in that day. "Therefore," David wrote, "the ungodly shall not stand in the judgment, nor sinners in the congregation of the righteous" (Ps. 1:5). No one who has not put his trust in Christ and forsaken the world shall be able to stand in that day.

Who shall be able to stand? The one who has put his trust in Christ, the one who has forsaken the world, the one who has overcome. What did he overcome? He overcame the temptation to quit. The devil comes along and says, "But you have been serving God now for 10 years, and you've had nothing but trouble. You have lost your job; your wife broke her leg; and your baby got diphtheria. Your car ran off the road and piled up, and you've never had anything but trouble since you started serving the Lord." We are tempted to listen to the blandishments of the devil and decide what to do. We stop going to prayer meeting and soon stop praying altogether.

That is the business of the devil. The man who knows God in reality does not listen to those blandishments. He says, "Naked came I out of my mother's womb, and naked shall I return thither" (Job 1:21). If God takes away everything I have, I will love Him anyhow. I will praise Him even if He slays me. We have to overcome, because the overcomer will be able to stand in that day, that terrible, terrible day.

This is only a summation of things, and I certainly have not given all the details. But I want to pose one question: Who shall be able to stand? Are you among them? If not, you might as well not have been born. However, it is so easy to become one who is able to stand. We must turn from our wicked ways unto Jesus Christ our Lord and become one of those protected and shielded forever and ever, guaranteed by the Lamb of God.

I Dreamed that the Great Judgment Morning

Bertram H. Shadduck (1869–1950)

I dreamed that the great judgment morning
Had dawned, and the trumpet had blown;
I dreamed that the nations had gathered
To judgment before the white throne;
From the throne came a bright, shining angel,
And he stood on the land and the sea,
And he swore with his hand raised to Heaven,
That time was no longer to be.

And, oh, what a weeping and wailing,
As the lost were told of their fate;
They cried for the rocks and the mountains,
They prayed, but their prayer was too late.

The rich man was there, but his money
Had melted and vanished away;
A pauper he stood in the judgment,
His debts were too heavy to pay;
The great man was there, but his greatness,
When death came, was left far behind!
The angel that opened the records,
Not a trace of his greatness could find.

The widow was there with the orphans,
God heard and remembered their cries;
No sorrow in heaven forever,
God wiped all the tears from their eyes;
The gambler was there and the drunkard,

And the man that had sold them the drink,
With the people who gave him the license,
   Together in hell they did sink.

The moral man came to the judgment,
   But self-righteous rags would not do;
The men who had crucified Jesus
   Had passed off as moral men, too;
The soul that had put off salvation,
   "Not tonight; I'll get saved by and by,
No time now to think of religion!"
   At last they had found time to die.

13

THE ETERNAL BLESSEDNESS OF THE BLESSED HOPE

Dear Lord Jesus, we are between heaven and hell in this spinning world. Our time is short, our days few and we so much need Thee. Thou hast put a light in the dark place that we might not be as those who sleep in the night, but that we might know and be awake, informed and alert. We pray Thou wilt help us, O God, in hearing. May we have ears to hear. We have heard men until we are weary. Men who know not whereof they speak, speaking of that whereof they know nothing. Thou, God, knowest all things. Speak, Lord, to our hearts. May we hear a voice that is Thy voice, and be conscious that we are listening to a proclamation, a trumpet, a voice. Great God, make it so. Amen.

In previous chapters, we saw our Lord opening the sixth seal, which indicated war, famine and plagues, and we saw the souls of the martyrs underneath the altar, in the hands of God. There was the shaking of heaven and earth, which affected the sun, moon, stars, mountains, islands and all humanity. Now comes a breathing spell between the sixth and the seventh seal.

John is still looking through the open door, and he sees "four angels standing on the four corners of the earth" (Rev. 7:1). Some who attack the Bible do so in this area of the four corners. Critics have tried to point out that it is obvious that the person who wrote this book believed the earth was square or at least flat. The critic says that a knowledgeable man could not have written this Bible, because he talked about the four corners of the earth.

Those who possess any kind of sense understand what John meant. When he wrote about the four corners of the earth, he was talking about the four cardinal points: North, South, East and West. Even apart from the Scriptures, people talk about the four winds of heaven. The North wind, the South wind, the East wind and the West wind; and they whirl all around and come at you from any angle. Those are the major winds, and that is all it means here. The angels stood on the four corners of the earth, holding the four winds of heaven.

The Activity of God's Holy Angels

The book of Revelation alone mentions angels 75 times; anything mentioned that much in one book of the Bible should not be skipped over. If I believe in the Bible, and the Bible mentions angels 75 times in one book, I need to have my eyes open a little bit and say to myself, *Wait a minute here. Maybe we have skipped lightly over something that needs to be taken seriously or at least looked into.*

The Bible as a whole talks about angels, mentioning them 297 times. A few times, the word "angel" in our English Bible refers to a human messenger, for the word means "messenger"; but the vast majority of times, it refers to a being from heaven. That being is usually large, powerful, immortal, holy, wise and closely associated with God. Jesus our Lord said about angels that they do not marry and are not given in marriage. Neither can they die; so they are immortal, holy and wise. They go back and forth doing the errands of the Almighty.

I am going to skip mentioning anything about fallen angels, for I do not know much about them. I probably know as much as I want to know. I am writing about the holy angels. These angels are always on the side of righteousness and God, and usually on the side of man. I say "usually" because there have been occasions when angels could not go along with man because of sin and rebellion. When God sends them to be ministers to men, they are naturally on the side of man.

I notice that in the Scriptures the angels are more active in times of crisis and less apparent in quieter times. In Job 38:4, God describes to Job the dawn of creation and asks, "Where wast thou when I laid the foundations of the earth?" Even though Job was not there, the angels were. It was such a spectacular event that God says, "When the morning stars sang together . . . all the sons of God shouted for joy" (v. 7).

It was when God was giving the Law that He gave it to the mediation of angels. The angels were active then. When our Lord came into the world and was born of a woman, the angels were seen then—there was a great multitude of the heavenly host praising God and saying, "Glory to God on high." Later on, when our Lord had risen from the dead, the angels were there again.

When you get to the book of Revelation, and the crisis begins to churn and gets tighter and fiercer, the angels appear 75 times in that one book.

Why We Seldom Consider the Angels

The question I must pose is why modern evangelical Christians have little place for angels in their thinking. Everybody else talks about angels, usually in the wrong connotation, but modern-day Christians do not talk much about angels.

Perhaps the basic reason is that the veil of materialism is on the modern religious mind. We have linked Christ with earthly prosperity. We equate Christianity with prosperity; consequently, we have no place for angels. You cannot buy or sell an angel. He is not going to bring you anything, especially good luck.

Our modern materialistic mind says that when the man who is making money is a Christian, the Lord is his co-partner. What I want to know is, when he is not making any money, is he still a Christian? If I read my Bible right, that is upside down with the Scriptures. We read in the Scriptures that the rich man was having a tough time getting to heaven, and the poor man went sailing through quite easily (see Matt. 19:24). So I think we had better rethink this whole deal, for I believe we are badly off center.

We Have Muted the Supernatural

The reason behind all of this is that popular Bible teaching has denied, or at least muted, the supernatural. The idea of the immediacy of God, and the necessity of God, is not found in many places. In fact, we get worried when God becomes necessary to us.

As soon as the supernatural becomes necessary to us, we are miserable. We want to know the supernatural is out there somewhere, farther than the farthest rock, but we also want to wring all of the goodies out of this world that we can. We want to squeeze every hive of honey and wring every bit of sweetness out of it. Then, when we are so old, battered and calcified that we could not enjoy ourselves anyhow, we want to go to that supernatural place. In the meantime, we would rather God did not bother us, because trusting the supernatural is an edgy, sensitive thing we do not want to do.

A preacher has to fight that same temptation. It is a sad thing when we have denied or muted the supernatural to a point where we have confined every miracle to another dispensation.

Our Roots Are Too Deeply in the Earth

The four angels standing at the four corners of the earth, holding back the four winds, is one of the most wonderful scenes I have ever read about or seen with my mind's eye. These angels are holding the winds of heaven as though God is dramatically waiting. You know what God is doing? I have been writing about it since the fifth chapter. God is jarring the earth loose from humanity's control. Man has his roots in the earth and has deeply driven down his stakes. God says the earth does not belong to man; the earth belongs to the man, Christ Jesus. The only man who is worthy, who has earned His right to hold the earth, He is now shaking the earth loose. I am very happy for this, and I will be glad when all these crises are over.

Nobody owns a thing; we just think we do. There is only one that owns it; He is the one who bled for it and gave Himself. The earth belongs to Him, and God is going to shake it loose so that nobody can say, "This is mine." God is going to turn it back over to the one to whom it belongs, the one who carries around with Him the form of a man and whose body was made of the very elements the earth gave Him.

The four angels are holding the four winds of heaven; and God is waiting now for the four winds to begin their destructive work on the earth to help jar the earth loose from man's control.

We Ascribe Cookie-Cutter Uniformity to Heaven

An angel comes out with the seal of God, cries out with a loud voice and speaks to these four angels; evidently, he is capable of giving orders to these four angels. That means that there are gradations of angels. The idea of cookie-cutter uniformity in heaven is one of the greatest errors and heresies I know. The Bible says that in heaven men shall differ from each other as star is different from star in glory. The Bible talks about angels, archangels, principalities, powers, might and dominions. That tells us there are gradations or lesser and greater authority. The idea that everybody is put in a sack and shaken up and all come out exactly alike is wrong.

There are going to be degrees in heaven. There are going to be rewards—some big, some little, some not at all. There are going to be people who have earned the right by their sufferings and tears to rule over five cities. Others get in only by the skin of their teeth, so as by fire. The idea that everybody who is born again is equal to everybody else that is born again is just as silly as it is possible to be.

There are differences in abilities and size and so forth. Here is one angel who has authority over these four angels, and he says, "Hurt not the earth, neither the seam nor the trees, till we have sealed the servants of our God in their foreheads" (Rev. 7:3). This sealing is not an unusual thing; at least it is not unprecedented:

> He cried also in mine ears with a loud voice, saying, "Cause them that have charge over the city to draw near, even every man with his destroying weapon in his hand." And, behold, six men came from the way of the higher gate, which lieth toward the north, and every man a slaughter weapon in his hand; and one man among them was clothed with linen, with a writer's inkhorn by his side: and they went in, and stood beside the brazen altar. And the glory of the God of Israel was gone up from the cherub, whereupon he was, to the threshold of the house. And he called to the man clothed with linen,

which had the writer's inkhorn by his side; And the LORD said unto him, "Go through the midst of the city, through the midst of Jerusalem, and set a mark upon the foreheads of the men that sigh and that cry for all the abominations that be done in the midst thereof" (Ezek. 9:1-4).

The Angels Will Seal the Remnant

In Revelation 7, we read that the angels seal the servants of God on their foreheads: "There were sealed an hundred and forty and four thousand of all the tribes of the children of Israel" (v. 4).

The Remnant Is on the Earth

Who are the 144,000? The cults point to themselves as the answer. What right do I have, or anybody else, for that matter, to make a figure or symbol out of anything as clear? God says who these are and names them. They are connected with the Hebrew remnant. They are people saved out of the 12 tribes of Israel; and in case someone might think it is something else, He names the tribes, including Joseph, for Ephraim. These Jews will be converted then.

Not all the judgments of God coming upon the earth at that time will affect these people. Do not ask me whether I believe or know if present Israel is the Israel spoken of here. I do not know for sure about that. However, I do know that Israel will come from the North and the South, the East and the West, and they will be restored again to the land God gave to Abraham, Isaac and Jacob. God never lied to Abraham. When God said Abraham could have the land from the river to the sea to the Cedars of Lebanon down to the borders of Egypt and Arabia, He meant exactly what He said.

The Great Multitude Is in Heaven

"After this I beheld," John writes, "and, lo, a great multitude, which no man could number, of all nations, and kindreds, and people, and tongues, stood before the throne, and before the Lamb, clothed with white robes, and palms in their hands" (v. 9).

Here is another multitude that cannot be numbered. This multitude is before the throne in heaven. The 144,000 are in earth. These in heaven, in contrast, are from all nations of the earth. Who are they? They are those who have come out of the great tribulation—the afflictions, anguish and persecution that are coming upon this world.

There is much controversy about the tribulation—when it takes place and when it starts. Here is something we can know: The ones mentioned here are saved out of the earth's iron furnace, no doubt, during a period yet future.

If you think you can untangle things so that you will understand them in the world today and know whose side to be on, who is right, who is wrong, think again. You cannot do it. If you think you are going to be able to explain why one man is rich and atheistic and another man is poor and holy; why one person lives to be 97 years old, and a woman dies of cancer in her 30s; if you think you can figure it all out, you are certainly going to be disillusioned.

This one thing you can do: When you reach a place where you cannot get the answer, you can look up and say, "Blessing, and glory and wisdom and thanksgiving, and honor, and power, and might, be unto our God for ever and ever. Amen" (Rev. 7:12). If you keep on saying that long enough, your heart will leap up, and you will be on top of things even if you cannot explain them. We can praise God for things even if we never can explain them.

A Radical Reduction of the Earth's Population

"One of the elders answered, saying unto me, What are these which are arrayed in white robes? and whence came they?" Although John certainly knows more than any of us will ever know, he said, "Sir, thou knowest" (vv. 13-14).

There is a frightful tribulation coming—a time of violence and suffering and terror; a time of upset of nations and dislocation and pain. This is the time when God Almighty will shake the earth worse than an earthquake. Then there is going to be a radical reduction of the earth's population, as found here in the book of Revelation. That radical reduction of the earth's population is not going to be the result of anything man does. It is going to be from heaven itself.

In the seventh chapter, we read of God's angels holding the four winds of the earth so that the wind shall not blow on the seas, the earth or trees. God Almighty is doing that. Then we come to the eighth chapter and see God hurling down fire on the earth, and hail and fire mingled with blood. It is not anything to do with what man can possibly do.

Even now, we are hearing politicians, sociologists and scientists say that there are too many people in the earth. Something must be done to shut off the stream of human beings that are being born into the world. What utter confusion! Nobody knows the answer. These people are more confused than the cults. (Maybe I should call them the scientific cult.) At any rate, in that day, there will be a radical reduction of the earth's population.

The Bible does not hesitate to say that one-third of the people of the earth will be slain in an instant. This is not the result of nuclear fission or anything of that sort; rather, it is the work of God Almighty. The human race will survive this radical reduction.

How Does This Knowledge Affect Us Now?

Now, here is what bothers me: Christianity is not costing us much at all. Every evangelical who claims to be born again and have eternal life forever is not doing as much to propagate his faith as the cults do. The cults give more, do more, sacrifice more and put us to shame by their zeal and effort to make converts.

I believe it is time for us to rise up, get out of our rut and routine and begin to take our Christian faith seriously. If Christians were to take this whole thing dead seriously and dare to kneel down before God and say, "Oh God, I hereby give myself and my family and my business to Thee. Take it, Lord. Take me; and if it's necessary that, for Thy sake, I should lose everything, let me lose it, Lord. I'll pay the price, but I want to be all I ought to be."

If just one church full of people would get that serious, you would never hear the last of it. The news would go everywhere, like birds on a wing, and there would be such a revival, such a renaissance of New Testament believers as you could not dream possible. May God deliver us from the easygoing, smooth, comfortable, fat, oily Christianity that always is careful never to let the truth get hold of us and embarrass us. It cost the early saints everything. What is it costing us?

Day of Judgment! Day of Wonders!
John Newton (1725–1807)

Day of judgment! Day of wonders,
Hark! the trumpet's awful sound,
Louder than a thousand thunders,
Shakes the vast creation round!
How the summons will the sinner's heart confound!

See the Judge, our nature wearing,
Clothed in majesty divine!
You who long for His appearing
Then shall say, "This God is mine!"
Gracious Savior, own me in that day for Thine!

At His call the dead awaken,
Rise to life from earth and sea;
All the powers of nature shaken
By his look, prepares to flee.
Careless sinner, what will then become of thee!

Horrors, past imagination,
Will surprise your trembling heart,
When you hear your condemnation,
"Hence, accursed wretch, depart!
Thou, with Satan and his angels, have thy part!"

Satan, who now tries to please you,
Lest you timely warning take,
When that word is past, will seize you,
Plunge you in the burning lake:
Think, poor sinner, thy eternal all's at stake.

But to those who have confessed,
Loved and served the Lord below,
He will say, "Come near, ye blessed,
See the kingdom I bestow;
You forever shall my love and glory know."

14

THE MANIFESTATION OF THE BLESSED HOPE

Forgive us, O God, for being at ease in Zion when all around us are Thy warnings. We have been too engrossed in luxuries and pleasures to listen to the voice of the Blessed Hope. O God, may we hear with our ears what the Spirit is saying and then bring our lives into complete obedience with that message. Amen.

When the seventh seal is opened, the man of God said, "There was silence in heaven about the space of half an hour" (Rev. 8:1). Much speculation has been given to the significance of this silence.

I honestly do not know what this means. I have discovered that what we do not know often becomes material for sermons or teaching. Speculation is a wonderful way to hold the attention of some rather shallow-thinking people. I refuse to preach or write about that of which I know nothing, and I know little about this except that there was a pause here in heaven, perhaps a sort of Selah, like we see in the psalms. To be perfectly frank, nobody knows what it really means. It may be a musical notation, but we really do not know.

What we do know is that God is working and the seals are being opened; and when the seventh seal is opened, there is a kind of divine Selah in heaven as those wheels of judgment are, for a little while, ground to a merciful stop. After the passing of that half-hour space, John writes, "I saw the seven angels which stood before God; and to them were given seven trumpets" (v. 2). The seven angels are pointed out here as being something special for the occasion. They were given the seven trumpets, indicating that God was giving these special seven trumpets to these special angels for a purpose. There were other trumpets throughout the Word of God, but these special trumpets were about to sound.

I've noticed something here that I have never thought of before. Another angel came and stood at the altar, which would be the divine altar in heaven. This scene evidently takes place in heaven, and the angel stands at the altar. This angel, or messenger of God, probably was sent from the throne of God. Some would even think it was Christ Himself, but there was given to this one a golden censer; and there was given unto him much incense that he should offer it with the prayers of all saints upon the golden altar before the throne. The earth is waiting, and God is watching the cup of iniquity fill up, and the people of God are praying, "O God, Thy kingdom come, Thy will be done." Back in the sixth chapter, the souls under the altar have been praying, "Oh Lord, holy and true; how long?" And the saints on earth have been in prayer, asking that the kingdom of God might come on earth.

That prayer cannot be answered unless there is first the judgment of God to shake loose the earth from the usurpers who now hold it and give it back to the Son of God to whom it belongs. He is the one who created it and who bought it back with His own precious blood. The prayers of the saints were upon the golden altar, but they were, for the time, ineffective.

Our Prayers Linked with God's Judgment

There are times when the prayers of the saints seem ineffective, that is, they are held for a while. In Revelation 8 we read that the prayers of all the saints have gone up to God upon the altar where they are kept and then mixed with prayer from off the altar or with incense, much incense. When the prayers of Christ, from the altar, were mixed with the prayers of the saints, living and dead, then the smoke of the incense ascended up before God, and the angel took the censer and filled it with fire off of the altar. The earth will not have the talons of the usurper shaken loose from it until there is judgment and the fire off of the altar.

Men like to believe this nation or another, this army or that army, this weapon or that weapon, this bomb or that bomb is going to hold a balance of power and determine the situation. But the outcome of all things will be determined not by the nuclear bombs of men or armies or generals or summit conferences or general assemblies of nations, but from the prayers of the saints.

Every time a soul prays in the Holy Ghost, "Thy kingdom come, Thy will be done," that prayer is registered before God. The conditions down here in the world have iced over and piled snow up on those prayers for the time being. But the time is coming when God will pour out incense with the prayers of the saints, and the effective prayer of Jesus Christ will join with the effectual prayer of righteous men. Then He will pour out of that censer fire on the altar upon the earth, and there will be voices, thunder, lightning and an earthquake. Then the seven angels, which are the seven trumpets, prepare themselves to sound. Why are they sounding the trumpets? They are sounding the trumpets in order to announce to humanity that there is another world than earth.

The Bible mentions trumpets 125 times. In ancient Israel, trumpets served as a bugle in the Army. As the Army camp is always within sound of the bugle, so in the wilderness it could always be heard. In Israel's camp, the bugle could be heard all over the camp. Different calls meant different things.

Israel would hear a call that was the sound of the alarm, and another call that was a call to assembly. Another call was the call to the feast. Another call was a call to war. Another call sounded forth the day of Jubilee. The prophets carried that figure over and used it: "Blow ye the trumpet in Zion, and sound an alarm in my holy mountain: Let all the inhabitants of the land tremble: for the day of the Lord cometh, for it is nigh at hand" (Joel 2:1). Paul used it in the New Testament when he said, "For if the trumpet give an uncertain sound, who shall prepare himself to the battle?" (1 Cor. 14:8). On Mount Sinai, the trumpet of God sounded amidst darkness, earthquakes, thunder and lightning. And in judgment, we read of this very thing:

> And then shall appear the sign of the Son of man in heaven: and then shall all the tribes of the earth mourn, and they shall see the Son of man coming in the clouds of heaven with power and great glory. And he shall send his angels with a great sound of a trumpet, and they shall gather together his elect from the four winds, from one end of heaven to the other (Matt. 24:30-31).

"In a moment, in the twinkling of an eye," the apostle Paul writes, "at the last trump: for the trumpet shall sound, and the dead shall be raised incorruptible, and we shall be changed" (1 Cor. 15:52). This refers, of course, to the seven trumpets in Revelation 8. That is the scriptural setting for it all; and when it carries over to this book of Revelation, it comes not as a new thing introduced, but as something with which any Bible student is familiar.

Those Who Have Ears to Hear

Notice the reasons for the trumpets of judgment. God once walked and talked with men and spoke to them in the quiet voice of love. He spoke in the cool of the day and they heard His voice as the voice of love walking among the trees of the garden. Man can no longer hear or will not hear that soft voice of God, because he has sinned.

In the Old Testament, Elijah discovered that God does not often speak in a very dramatic way. After the great victory on Mount Carmel, Elijah feared Queen Jezebel, and ran and hid in the cave. It was in that cave that God came to Elijah, not in the thunder or the earthquake, but in a still, small voice:

> And he said, Go forth, and stand upon the mount before the LORD. And, behold, the LORD passed by, and a great and strong wind rent the mountains, and brake in pieces the rocks before the LORD; but the LORD was not in the wind: and after the wind an earthquake; but the LORD was not in the earthquake: And after the earthquake a fire; but the LORD was not in the fire: and after the fire a still small voice (1 Kings 19:11-12).

God has spoken, and He is speaking in many ways. He spoke by the prophets, by the seers, by reason, in nature, in the Scriptures; the Bible tells us that He spoke by holy men who were moved by the Holy Ghost: "God, who at sundry times and in divers manners spake in time past unto the fathers by the prophets" (Heb. 1:1). He has spoken through holy men who have lived and preached and prayed and sang since the Bible was written; and He spoke most loudly and most clearly in His Son, Jesus Christ our Lord:

[He] hath in these last days spoken unto us by his Son, whom he hath appointed heir of all things, by whom also he made the worlds; Who being the brightness of his glory, and the express image of his person, and upholding all things by the word of his power, when he had by himself purged our sins, sat down on the right hand of the Majesty on high (Heb. 1:2-3).

Sinning men, however, are not listening. Only an occasional believing ear will hear. "He that hath an ear," says the Holy Spirit, "let him hear" (Rev. 3:22).

In this hour of world agony, men have filled the cup of iniquity and rejected the Father and Son and Holy Ghost, and have fouled the beautiful earth, and then reached out to do the same to other worlds. Just as the cup of iniquity is about ready to brim over, God speaks to the seven trumpeters; they come forth and start blowing their trumpets. In that hour, the world will go over to the Antichrist, and he will enslave the major portion of the world and violate every natural and spiritual law. Even the judgments of God will be considered something else and explained away.

When God spoke out of heaven to His Son, the people around heard a voice and said, "It thundered." But it was the voice of God. Men are refusing to believe that God speaks, even when He speaks, because of unbelief. Science is explaining it all away. When you consider the amazing and terrifying things being done in the realm of biology, consider that it cannot be too many generations away that marriage may be abolished altogether from some countries and babies will be created in test tubes.

Instead of saying, "Listen, God is speaking," wise men are nervously adjusting their eyepiece and explaining it away. It is going to take the comfort of God to rouse us. It is going to take something out of this world; and when God shakes the world loose from her scientists, her politicians, her playboys and turns it over to the one to whom it belongs, Jesus Christ the Lord, He is going to do it in such a way that everybody will recognize it as a miraculous manifestation. The trumpets will confirm God's judgments.

We Need a Renewed Awe of Prophecy

Notice the first four trumpets. These four trumpets tell us that there will be unmistakable manifestations from heaven. All the prophets, our Lord Himself and His apostles all said so. I do not know that the time is upon us yet; I do know it is coming. We have talked about these things until we have reached a point of diminishing returns now. You can talk about a thing often enough, long enough, carelessly enough, spiritlessly enough, and soon you reach a point of diminishing returns, and it has no more effect and no more meaning. I believe that is what has happened to us who are evangelicals in this area of prophecy.

We are losing our ability to be afraid anymore. There is no awe left in the earth. It's like the old story of the boy that cried wolf when there was no wolf and cried it so often that he reached a point of diminishing returns. When he cried wolf when the wolf actually came, nobody listened to him, and the wolf stole all his sheep.

Christians hardly believe the prophets anymore. We are ignoring God now and ignoring the truth. How long since you read the prophets and even worried about their message? How long since you heard a real sermon on prophecy, the end times, the coming of the Lord and the winding up of this world?

If Noah had not believed in his hour, the human race would have been wiped out. If Noah had not believed when God spoke, the history of the Old Testament would be quite different. Thank God, one man believed. "Thou has found grace in my sight," said the Holy One to Noah. And Noah believed.

What if Lot had ignored the warning when the angels came down, took him by the arm and said, "Come, get out of here. Get thee away, for the fire is going to fall on Sodom and Gomorrah"? If Lot had ignored the warning, I am sure the world would have been a different world and the Scriptures would have been different. But Lot believed. He was not a very good man, but he believed enough to get up and get his family out of there. Knowing what his wife did afterwards, I imagine he had a hard time getting her away (see Gen. 19:23-29).

One of these days, when those mighty, awe-inspiring angels of God pick up the silver trumpets and blow, they will be heard among all the planets and stars and everywhere on the earth, and nobody can say it is thunder. They will know better.

Christians are at ease in Zion, engrossed in luxuries and pleasures, neglecting to pray; the result is that they do not hear the voice. Some say, "When I hear the trumpet, then I'll take care of things." When you hear the trumpet, it is going to be too late.

Scripture tells us there will be the seven trumpets, and when they start to blow, it will be too late. "Woe, woe, woe," to those who inhabit the earth, says the mighty voice. Then the last three trumpets are to sound (see Rev. 8:13).

There Is Still Time

Until that time, we are listening for another voice—the voice of Jesus calling us home. It is the gentle voice of Jesus saying, in this hour of man's hope and possibility and opportunity, "Come unto me, all ye that labour and are heavy laden" (Matt. 11:28). If we will not hear that voice, we may hear the voice of the trumpet. Christians must hear the voice of God saying that we are to beware lest we be overcome with surfeiting, drunkenness and the cares of this life, and so that day overtakes us unaware.

Right now, God is not calling men to Him with the trumpet. It is written of Him that He never cried aloud nor lifted up His voice, nor made it to be heard in the streets. He would send His messengers. Today He has sent the quiet voice of man. He has sent the beautiful, sweet voice of song. He has sent the personal worker, the evangelist, the quiet old pastor and the simple housewife who teaches a Sunday School class.

He has not yet sent the angel with the trumpet, and the voice we hear is not, "Woe, woe, woe." The voice we hear is, "Come unto me all ye that labor and are heavy laden and I will give you rest. Take my yoke upon you and learn from me for I am meek and lowly in heart and ye shall find rest unto your souls" (Matt. 11:28-29). The voice we hear is, "Awake thou that sleepest, and arise from the dead, and Christ shall give thee light" (Eph. 5:14). The voice we hear is, "Repent, repent."

The reason God has not yet sent judgment upon this earth is to give the inhabitants the time and opportunity to repent of their sins. It is an awesome, terrifying fact. Deal with your sin now, or your sin will deal with you later. All we have is now. When our "now" is exhausted, the trumpet of the Lord will sound.

When the Roll Is Called Up Yonder
James Milton Black (1856–1938)

When the trumpet of the Lord shall sound,
and time shall be no more,
And the morning breaks, eternal, bright and fair;

When the saved of earth shall gather
over on the other shore,
And the roll is called up yonder, Ill be there.

On that bright and cloudless morning
when the dead in Christ shall rise,
And the glory of His resurrection share;
When His chosen ones shall gather
to their home beyond the skies,
And the roll is called up yonder, I'll be there.

Let us labor for the Master
from the dawn till setting sun,
Let us talk of all His wondrous love and care;
Then when all of life is over,
and our work on earth is done,
And the roll is called up yonder, I'll be there.

When the roll, is called up yonder,
When the roll, is called up yonder,
When the roll, is called up yonder,
When the roll is called up yonder I'll be there.

15

THE WARNING OF THE BLESSED HOPE

*O blessed Lord Jesus, Thou didst come on a nation, our trembling
hearts tell us. Thou hast come with blazing eyes to be our judge.
Thou shouldest have come with our executioner to put to
death such moral vermin that has crawled all over the face of
the earth, pulling at each other and ourselves. Thou didst not come to
condemn the world but hast come that the world through
Thee might be saved. What can we say, Lord, but thank Thee, O gentle
Savior. How can we borrow language to thank Thee for this?
We thank Thee, Lord Jesus. We will not fight about Thee and we will
not argue about hypotheses. We will only kneel and say, "My Lord and
my God. We have found Him of whom Moses and the prophets did
write: Jesus, the Son of Mary, the Son of God. We have found Him!
Hallelujah! We have found Him." Amen.*

My method in this book has not been to interpret all the symbols, or to force every passage to fit into a pattern. To do so
would run the risk of spiritual dishonesty or of narrowing your
mind to a place where you can never expand or grow in the
Lord, and He cannot say anything further to you. My purpose
has been to identify the main points and discover the underly-
ing spiritual lessons.

The star in the first chapter of the book of Revelation is the
angel of the seven churches. I do not know who the star is in

Revelation 9, but I know that it came down from heaven unto the earth. Something supernatural invades our natural world. This stranger coming into the world is from another order of being and he holds in his hands the keys of the abyss, the bottomless pit. He opens it at the command of God. Out of this abyss come locusts upon the earth, which are not the kind of locusts the world has been used to seeing. These locusts had the power of a scorpion.

The Locusts

Scorpions on earth are few, but locusts come in droves—thousands and hundreds of thousands—and all they do is eat vegetation. They do not bother people; but if you were to give locusts the power of the scorpion, you can imagine what sort of torment you would have on your hands.

This description is of multiplied hundreds of thousands of locusts, every one of them with a sting like a scorpion. They were told not to hurt the vegetation of the earth, nor any of the people that had the seal of God in their foreheads, which shows us there were people and will be people who have God's seal in that day. The command was given that they should not kill the wicked people, but torment them with a torment so terrible that in those days men will seek death and not find it. They will try to commit suicide and will be unsuccessful. Death will flee from them. John tells us the shape of the locusts, and of course he is using figures of speech here.

The locusts are like horses prepared for battle. On their heads are crowns of gold, and their faces are as the faces of men. They have hair as women and their teeth are as the teeth of lions. I never saw a creature like this. But they will be here in that terrible day. The noise of their wings is like the sound of chariots with horses running to battle. They have tails like the scorpions, and they hurt man for a period of five months.

These locusts have a king over them. His name in Hebrew is Abaddon (destruction), and in Greek it is Apollyon (destroyer). That is the first thing that happens when the fifth angel sounds the trumpet. Take note of this: In God's economy, another world keeps an eye on this world. The world in which we live is neither self-explanatory nor self-sufficient. The world that we are so familiar with is but a shadow of the real world above. What many people fail to realize is that this world has a spiritual origin. However, a rebel race is usurping authority in this world and has, for the time being, separated itself from God's world in God's kingdom. The time is coming when God will settle this insurrection.

The Judgment of God

The book of Revelation reveals to us the way in which God is going to settle this rebel occupation of earth. Creatures from other worlds are moving in on this world. All through the Scriptures, the prophets and seers and sages, and even the apostles, warned us of what God has planned to do. All the rebellion that seems to go unchecked will one day meet its match, and more than its match. This rebellious world of ours, which has been a rebellious province, with all of its people rebelling against the High King of heaven, is coming back into the divine order again, and the unity of God's world will be restored and preserved.

God will bring to bear upon this evil infection the balances of His justice. In order to bring this about, there will be the opening of the seals, the sounding of the trumpets and the sound of the pouring out of the vials of God's wrath. God uses this to shake the rebellious world loose from the earth, or the earth from the rebellious world of humanity. These invaders in Revelation 9 will be from above and from below. The supernatural moves into the natural, and I would like to say that when that happens, everybody will know where the invaders came from, or at least that they come from another world.

When that invasion takes place, nobody will be writing articles and asking whether there is such a thing. God will make it very plain. Nobody will be telling weird stories about seeing little men getting out of a flying saucer. There will be no question that this is the judgment of God upon the world. Then God will send His strange creatures from hell and from heaven to invade the earth. Nobody will doubt or question it, but the sad truth is that they will not surrender—and they will not repent—even though they will know from whence it all came.

Now we see the picture only dimly and do not understand it all. A man writes a book to explain what the star is; another writes a book to explain that the man who wrote the first book did not know what he was talking about. Yet another man writes a book about the locusts, and another man writes a book to show that the man who wrote the first book about the locust had never seen a locust, and so it goes.

Although I am purposely not going to get involved in these details, I do know the great central truth here: When God gets enough of the world, He is going to do something about it. If you are close enough to God to want Him to do something about it, you are a good Christian. Most do not want Him to do anything about it. They secretly pray, "Oh, God, hold off Thy judgments." However, those close enough to God that their hearts beat with God's are crying, "Oh, God, send Thy judgments and let Thy judgments be revealed."

What We Can Know

In light of this, I want to lay out five truths that can be known. These truths are taught here, and I want you to examine them and think about them.

The Essential Nature of Earth

The first truth is that this world is essentially spiritual. This is what God has been saying to the world ever since Adam and Eve sinned. "I've made you," God pleads, "in My image." All this that we see came out of that which cannot be seen. This world did not jump into being of itself. It is not an accident. It was created out of spirit by the birth of God's breath, and man was made in God's image. The visible world is a manifestation of spirit; and since we only see external things, we misunderstand them.

It is like seeing a building designed for a purpose, and somebody comes along and says, "That building was not designed. That building just happened." Wait a minute. There are windows, doors, entrances, here and there. There are shapes of rooms inside, indicating that intelligence with a purpose in mind made that building.

Somebody objects. "No, we don't acknowledge that at all. We have no way of knowing. Nobody is in there. Let's go through it." They comb the building from top to bottom and find nothing. They find no evidence of life at all. No evidence that anything is in there, and they come out and triumphantly say, "There is nothing there. It just happened."

Somebody comes along who knows his right hand from his left and says, "There's every evidence here of design, every evidence of purpose, every evidence of intelligence, and we can't find it through seeing or feeling or hearing the one who made it, but somebody made it."

God is saying to the world that the world is essentially spiritual because He made it, and it came out of Him, and He breathed life into the world. That is why we are here; but men forget that. The scientists in particular forget that, and they make good on what they are saying because they appeal to your five senses. They can produce a microphone and amplify a voice. They can produce light to make it shine and do other evidences. We who believe in God and in His purpose and design have no proof of anything. We have to say, "I believe in God the Father Almighty. I believe in Jesus Christ, His only Son. I believe in the Holy Ghost. I believe in the holy catholic church. I believe."

The scientists serenely smile at us and say, "Well, we don't believe; we produce." While the world is producing their great instruments of death and of life, God is saying to the world not to get too serious about all of this. He is saying, "I made all of this. The world is essentially spiritual, and the springs of human conduct are spiritual. Even fleshly sins—however vile and violent—are the outflow of poisoned spiritual springs.

There Is More to Come

The second truth we can see here is that the world has not seen anything yet. This has been a harsh, violent, bloody, sinful, tear-stained, terror-filled world. Every newspaper comes out with it, every radio and television program tells us how terrible and harsh and violent and bloody it all is. That is the price we are paying for the monstrous inversion and the reckless rebellion against the High King of heaven. That is the price we are paying for forgetting that we are spiritual. It is the price we pay for going down to the beasts that perish and living such lives that are no longer true. That is the price we are paying for making the spirit to be a servant of the flesh.

I once saw a man take a candle and say, "This candle is like a man. Here is the candle—the body. The wick goes up the middle, which is the soul. At the top burns the flame, which is the spirit." Then he went on to explain that the candle will give light as long as it holds its right relative position. As long as the body is below, the soul is inside and the spirit is at the top, it will burn. Then he turned it over; as soon as he turned it over, there was a sputter and a puff of smoke, and the flame went out. He explained, "That comes from inverting it and putting the spirit down and the body up."

That is exactly what has happened to the world. We are living that kind of life today. We are body- and world-conscious to a point that we forget there should burn at the apex of our lives an everlasting flame that can never go out—the spirit of a man in touch with the Spirit of God. But we turn it over and the body puts out the spirit, and men die. Some cherish the vain hope that someday they will find a way to God.

I believe the world we are living in today is a mad world. This world is turned upside down and has forgotten they were made in the image of God. They have forgotten there is another world. They have forgotten there will be a day when God will invade the world with strange creatures from heaven above and earth beneath. These creatures from other worlds do the bidding of God and will race faster than the speed of light. They will go to God's earth and do their terrible, wonderful, awful judgment work.

The voice tells the sixth angel who blows the trumpet, "Loose the four angels which are bound in the great river Euphrates" (Rev. 9:14). The four angels were loosed, which were prepared for an hour, a day, a month and a year to slay a third part of men. I do not know who these creatures are, but I know the Scripture says something to the effect that they are bound by the River Euphrates, and God is going to loose them. When they come, everybody will know we have been visited.

Death Is Not the End

The third thing we know is that death is not the worst thing that can happen to a man. We do not understand this today, but it is true. In that day, men desire to die and cannot, and death shall flee from them. No Christian is afraid of death. The apostle Paul set this straight in his epistle:

> We are confident, I say, and willing rather to be absent from the body, and to be present with the Lord. Wherefore we labour, that, whether present or absent, we may be accepted of him. For we must all appear before the judgment seat of Christ; that every one may receive the things done in his body, according to that he hath done, whether it be good or bad. Knowing therefore the terror of the Lord, we persuade men; but we are made manifest unto God; and I trust also are made manifest in your consciences (2 Cor. 5:8-11).

Death for a Christian is a journey to the eternal world; and so it is a triumphant victory and a rest and delight. The apostle Paul was anxious to go. I understand how Paul felt a little bit. I have never suffered as Paul suffered. I suppose the more he suffered, the more he wanted to go to heaven. The more the Christian suffers, the more anxious he is for heaven and home.

Today's Christian has a different attitude about this. So many are so satisfied with everything they have that there is anxiousness about leaving it all behind. We are quite content with what we have and we pray, "Oh, God, please don't take me yet for a while. I like it here." Certainly, we do not pray that aloud, because it would not be pious to do it, but we live like that. How many Christians would be deeply disappointed if he thought God was going to take him to heaven today, tomorrow or the next day? He would plead, "Lord, please, hold the ball for a while. There are too many things I want here in this world."

For the Christian, death holds no fears; it is a journey to the eternal world. It is the reaching of that for which we were created. It is the sudden fulfillment of our purpose. How frightening could that ever be for the Christian whose anchor is deep in the heart and soul of Jesus Christ?

Death is not the worst thing that can happen to you, but failing God is. Here were these people crying for death. They shall seek death and shall not find it. They shall desire to die, and it shall flee from them. Death is not the worst thing that can happen to a man, because death is only the snuffing out of the body; but we live on.

God Controls the Destiny of All Men

The fourth thing that God is saying here is that He holds our lives in His hand. Hurt not them that have the seal of God in their foreheads. Men shall not find death, and it shall flee them, for those men have a certain freedom of the will. There will be times when God withholds His permission; and when He withholds His permission, the murderer cannot kill and the suicide cannot die.

We must deal with the world before us as a rebellious world. We believe in God and His Son, Jesus Christ; and if the world would listen to us, the solution to the world's problems would be right there. But they will not listen.

Not All Hearts Will Accept God's Call

The last thing I want to mention is that rebellious man cannot be forced to repent. The remaining men who were not killed by these plagues did not repent of the works of their hands that they should not worship devils and idols; neither did they repent of their murders or their sorcerers or their fornications or their evils. Men have said that if God should send His judgment in the earth, then men would fear.

The Scriptures tell us here that in that day of the last invasion, men will harden themselves and refuse to repent. Jesus said, "If they hear not Moses and the prophets, neither will they be persuaded, though one rose from the dead" (Luke 16:31). If they will not hear the Word of God, if they will not react to the Word of God favorably and dare to believe and repent, "they would not even though a man rose from the dead."

The human heart is a strange thing. An act of God that will make one man repent will make another man hate God. The same sermon that will bring one person weeping to an altar of prayer will send another one out, chin up, determined to have his own way. The human heart is wicked above all things and desperately wicked (see Jer. 17:9). God have mercy on us. This is what God is saying to us.

I believe this day is coming, even though I do not know when. The world will see these creatures, and the saints will be marked and protected for the little time they will yet be here; but the rest will be under the judgment of God. Instead of seeking God in the foxholes, they will harden themselves and repent not of the murders, sorceries and fornication.

All men are morally obligated to repent; and if they do not, they will perish. Yet men will not repent unless the goodness of God softens them. Here is our warning. Do not trust in something dramatic; because if they hear not Moses and the prophets, they will not hear nor believe should someone dramatically rise from the dead.

That Day of Wrath, That Dreadful Day
Thomas of Celano (c. 1200–1265)

The day of wrath, that dreadful day,
When heaven and earth shall pass away!
What power shall be the sinner's stay?
How shall he meet that dreadful day?

When, shriveling like a parched scroll,
The flaming heavens together roll,
And louder yet, and yet more dread,
Resounds the trump that wakes the dead?

Oh, on that day, that wrathful day,
When man to judgment wakes from clay,
Be thou, O Christ, the sinner's stay,
Though heaven and earth shall pass away.

16

The Little Book of the Blessed Hope

*Heavenly Father, Thy Word has been a lamp unto my feet and a light
unto my path. I have found Thy Word to be the way into Thy presence.
Beyond the sacred page of Thy Word, I seek Thy face, Lord. Amen.*

The book of Revelation is primarily the revelation of Jesus Christ,
but it is impossible to look straight at a bright star and see only
that bright star. Looking at a bright star, we see all the other stars
round about it that are large enough and bright enough to reg-
ister on our optic nerves. It is impossible to see a king or to look
at a king without seeing other things around the king—the
palace and the throne and the attendants and the scepter and the
robe and the things that go to make the king a king.

When reading the book of Revelation, we often do not, for
the moment, see Jesus Himself; we see that which surrounds
Him. Jesus Christ is first. He is the Word, the everlasting Word.
He is God incarnated in human flesh.

I could spend a lot of time writing about Him, and yet I
would be ashamed of how little I would say in praise of Him
who is the desire of nations; about He who is the wisdom and
the righteousness and the sanctification and the redemption

and the hope and the resurrection and the glory; He who is the way and the truth and the life, and all that the human spirit will need, and all that we as human beings will need for the world to come. Yet, when we look toward Him, we see these other creatures too. Jesus is the one by whom the race is to be redeemed, the earth restored and evil vanquished. He is the one by whom Satan is defeated, justice established, the human banishment ended and the veil taken away from the face of God. Yet, when we gaze upon Him, we see angels, hell, heaven, the bottomless pit, the throne of God, the souls of the righteous, the last judgment, the marriage of the Lamb and the new heavens and the new earth.

Clothed with a Cloud

The book of Revelation is rich with wonderful scenes that are noble and magnificent, terrible and awesome, attractive and frightening and rapturous. John writes, "I saw another mighty angel come down from heaven clothed with a cloud. And a rainbow upon his head and his face as it were as the sun and his feet as pillars of fire" (Rev. 10:1).

The tenth chapter of Revelation is parenthetical, that is, it does not advance the progress of events. We are moving forward in the schedule of the events, but here we do not find any forward motion at all; but we see a loud and lordly announcement coming from another mighty angel. Then follows the description of the angel, and the Scripture says he is clothed with a cloud.

The Bible was written to a considerable degree in figures of speech and symbolism, which abounds throughout the Word of God. This often discourages some people, and they throw up their hands and say, "I cannot understand the Scriptures. I don't know when it's a literal thing and when it's a symbolic thing. Therefore, I just don't read the Word." That of course is the devil's neat trick to prevent us from reading the Word of God.

When you are reading a letter from a relative or a loved one who is far away, you have no such trouble. That loved one may use brilliant figures of speech in that letter to you. Yet, you know what every one of them means and you know your loved one is using a symbol—a figure of speech. You do not say, "I'll not read that letter because it talks about things I don't understand." You understand all right. So when we read of the angel clothed with the cloud, we know that this cloud, if we are Bible students, is not a rain cloud. It is not a cloud composed of water; it is some other kind of cloud.

Back in the days of Israel, there was a cloud by day and a fire glowing by night. It was the Shekinah of God's presence (the glory of God). And when Jesus was taken away, a cloud received Him out of the disciples' sight. Again, it says, "Behold, he cometh with clouds; and every eye shall see him, and they also which pierced him" (Rev. 1:7). This is what the cloud means; it is the visible manifestation and the setting forth of the glory of the invisible God.

When the creature comes out from the throne of God, there clings to him something of the glory belonging to God, something of the splendor and beauty that belong to God. The throne of God clings to the mighty angel as he moves down from his place by the throne of God to the place where he is coming on the earth. Around him is the majestic aura of God's presence.

Although this mighty angel is not Jesus Christ our Lord, Christ is seen through all of this. Our Lord is called the angel of the covenant in one place, but since the word "angel" means a messenger, this angel in the tenth chapter is another mighty messenger coming down from heaven, clothed with a cloud.

The Seven Thunders

I do not know about this little book (scroll) in Revelation 10, and so I am not going to emphasize it too much. I believe God keeps books on His people. I read of the Book of Life and the Book of Deeds, in which are written the evil works of men. I read in Revelation 5 about the title deed to the world. Therefore, the great God of heaven keeps books. And here is a little book, which the angel has in his hand. We may notice a little later what it is, but he cries with a loud voice.

He lifted up his hand to heaven. I like somebody or some creature that can do something with finality. We nibble at things; we experiment and try. We are weak; and we try to do things and do not get them done. "We're such little men when the stars come out," said the poet Hermann Hagedorn. But here is someone who comes down, lifts up his hand and cries with a loud voice; that is, he shouts as when a lion roars. When he had cried, seven thunders uttered their voices. Those seven thunders uttered something intelligible to John. John grabbed his quill pen and started to write down what the seven thunders uttered:

> I was about to write: and then I heard a voice from heaven saying unto me, Seal up those things, which the seven thunders uttered and write them not. And the angel which I saw stand upon the sea and upon the earth lifted up his hand to heaven, and sware by him that liveth for ever and ever, who created heaven, and the things that therein are, and the earth, and the things that therein are, and the sea, and the things which are therein, that there should be time no longer (vv. 4-6).

We make a great deal out of time being no more. In our hymns and gospel songs, we sing about looking forward to the day or the period when time will be no more; but actually, what the great angel, this mighty resplendent being, said here was that delay should be no longer.

We understand this if we are at a football or a baseball game. All somebody needs to do is to call "time" and everything ends. Nobody can score, nobody can run, nobody can do anything. They say, "Wait a minute, there is a delay in the game." Therefore, the sequence of the game ends for a while, and there is a parenthesis, a period of waiting. This is what we have now in the book of Revelation. We are in a period of waiting, when suddenly this great angel appears from heaven above and cries to the earth and to all that time is no longer called; the delay should not be long.

Faith Is Tested When "Time" Is Called

This is a great test of faith for the world, but also a great obstacle, too, when God has promised so much. Read your Bible. Go back to Genesis and read it on through and see how much God has promised through prophet, saint, sage, seer, apostle and our Lord Himself, but time has been called. The great test of faith is if we can wait on God, not push it and expect immediate results and action.

We live in the push-button age now. We live in that period when we want things done immediately. A man used to be able to wait for a day or two, or maybe a week, on a stagecoach. Now he is impatient if he misses one section of a revolving door. We want what we want now, and we do not want anybody fooling about it. God does not move like that, and faith does not always get things immediately.

The difference between faith as it is found in the Scriptures and faith as we conceive it is that to us, faith is a kind of magic. We want something and we pray, and we exercise faith and reach out, and we have that right now. When we pray, some things do come now; but there is another kind of long-range telescopic faith that sees the ages, and it can wait on God. The churches had to wait a long, long time. God has promised so many things, and His people have waited so very long, and their cry has gone up, "How long, O Lord, how long?"

Now the lordly angel proclaims with a voice as of a lion, and three worlds hear him. Heaven hears him and agrees; hell hears him and is frightened; earth hears him and is glad. "You won't have to wait any longer now," says this mighty angel, because "time is no more." Delay is no more; we are lifting the "time" signal from the game. Now we go forward to the end without any more delay.

God promised Abraham many things that He has not yet fulfilled. Abraham died without seeing it all and was buried in the cave of Machpelah, and later laid to rest beside the withered body of his wife Sarah. The dust of Abraham and Sarah still blows about over there somewhere, perhaps in Asia Minor, the land that God gave to Abraham, Isaac and Jacob. God said, "Abraham, I'll bless the whole earth through you and through your seed. I will give you all this land from way up here at the top, clear down, and from the river clear from the sea, clear out to beyond the river. I'll give it all to you."

There never has been a time when the descendants of Abraham had all that. They have had some of it, and they have had less of it and more of it; but they have never had all of it. So, Abraham is still waiting. God has said, "Abraham, we have to call 'time' a little here, and delay a bit. I'm going to let the tree ripen." Abraham has been waiting; but Abraham can afford to wait. The man, who when he was 100 years old could quietly look up to

God and believe that his wife, who was 90, could have a child, has no trouble with faith. Isaac was born in faith, in the will of God.

Then there was David. Oh, how God loved David! David was a human being and acted like one under pressure. David had known one art that the average human being does not know—the glorious art of repentance. He could repent as few men have ever been able to repent since the world began. David could sin in a robust fashion, but he could also weep as few men.

Most of the messianic psalms tell us about the King in His glory, coming to sit on His throne, and the people of the world gathering up to the King, and peace being throughout all the earth. That is not simply poetry; that is history prewritten. God has said that it would be.

We see it here, and we see it ahead of time, which is history prewritten. "For David speaketh concerning him, I foresaw the Lord always before my face, for he is on my right hand, that I should not be moved: Therefore did my heart rejoice, and my tongue was glad; moreover also my flesh shall rest in hope: Because thou wilt not leave my soul in hell, neither wilt thou suffer thine Holy One to see corruption. Thou hast made known to me the ways of life; thou shalt make me full of joy with thy countenance" (Acts 2:25-28).

Peter said, "My brethren, know that David died and sleeps now. That all the house of Israel know it, that David sleeps" (see Acts 2:29). Has God forgotten David? Isaiah, the man with the organ voice, who could pull out all the stops and make the heavens hear the great tunes as he told of Him who is Wonderful, Counselor, the Everlasting Father of the Prince of Peace, and that He should come and that the law should go out from Jerusalem, and the Word of the Lord should go out from Zion and the nations of the earth should come to Israel. Do you think God has forgotten these promises He made through Isaiah?

Daniel prayed his way through, fasted and sought the will and knowledge of God. Do you think this man, to whom God promised there would be a stone come out of heaven and strike the earth, and the stone should grow until it should fill the whole mountain? Do you suppose God has forgotten all this? We have forgotten it. We have got our minds made up on something else.

I think of the Church, and the only way we will know where we are is to know Church history a little bit. Everybody ought to buy a book on Church history, if only a synopsis. Then I recommend the reading of the biographies of the saints. It is a good cure for any new ideas that pop up. It is good to study and see how the Church, and particularly the martyrs, died in calm belief that everything would be all right in their Father's house. They are still waiting. God says, "Time," and they are waiting.

Now, in Revelation 10, it comes. "And the angel which I saw stand upon the sea and upon the earth lifted up his hand to heaven and sware by him that liveth for ever and ever, who created heaven and the things that are therein and the earth and the things that are therein and the sea and the things that are therein" (vv. 5-6). He swore that there should be time no more. Delay was over and now the wheel of God's justice rolls on.

The cup of wrath was filling up. That happens to human beings. We sin and sin and sin, and we think perhaps God does not notice much or at least He does not seem to. But the sin becomes accumulative. When it piles up to the place where it overflows, then the judgment of God falls.

The nations of the earth have been accumulating their sins. There was a day when the cup of wrath was filling up for the world, and the just judgment of God was about to fall; and then the saving victim opened wide the gates of heaven and gave Himself to die. He offered Himself on a cross, and God called "time" and said while My Son pleads at My right hand, and while grace is operative, there will be no end to the human race. There will be no final judgment. You and I are living now in a period when "time" has been called, but the great angel is coming.

Why God Has Still Called "Time"

I do not know how soon the angel will come, but he will come, and he will say, "Time is no more. The delay has ended" (see Rev. 10:6). The wheels will begin to roll on, and during this time, God is taking out of the world a people for His name.

The Church cannot be a religious theater where paid men perform for the religious amusement of the people who pay them. The Church is an assembly of redeemed people who have been called out and they are called by His own name. Moreover, He is taking out of the world a people for His name, and time waits while grace operates.

The Lord says He will call out of the nations a people for His name, and after that, He will return. I am going to believe that. I am not going to let anybody argue me out of that. I believe that is true. Soon, time will be no more; and when it is no more, then our Lord will come back; and when He comes back again, the big question will be, are we ready for His coming? I do not believe we are automatically ready.

We Still Have Time to Get Ready

I believe our Lord is waiting, but one of these times, that mighty angel with the loud voice is going to come down from God's heaven above with a rainbow upon his head and his face as the sun and his feet as pillars of fire. He is going to stand on the sea and on the land and lift up his hand to heaven and swear that the delay is over; and then God is going to begin to judge a world ill-prepared for judgment; a world all bogged down in iniquity. A world more concerned with games and pleasures than with getting ready to meet God.

A Bride is now being prepared for our Lord, in a secret place. The idea that there is an automatic legal aspect, that if you have your citizenship in heaven, you are all ready, I do not believe for a second. God is not going to allow His carnal, lustful, money-loving, pleasure-loving children to go rushing pellmell, singing gospel boogie, into the presence of the holy God. Something radical must take place to shake them loose from their carnal appetites.

The God who is holy said, "Be ye holy, for I am holy" (1 Pet. 1:16). I believe that God is going to prepare His people, and He is going to say to them, "Take a bath. Not with soap and detergent and water, but in the blood of Jesus Christ, as of a Lamb without spot and without blemish." No matter how much of a con artist a man is, he can push his way into religious circles these days and make good and succeed. Even though he is a fraud, he can do it. We can set our jaw and push our way in, but there is one place where you will not push your way in. I am glad there is one holy place where you cannot be permitted to get away with anything.

Do not ask me what the seven thunders uttered, because they were sealed up (see Rev. 10:4). Nobody knows what the seven thunders said. But you can know one thing: whatever they said, they did not say anything in favor of the devil or in favor of sin or hell, nor of the proud man. And you can be sure that whatever they said was said in favor of God and Christ and righteousness and holiness.

I am willing to wait for God to unloose the seven seals when John will say, "Now, here's what the seven thunders uttered." But with 66 books of the Bible, I am not too much worried about what the seven thunders uttered; I am very much concerned that I should be prepared when the wheels of judgment start to grind again and the cup of iniquity gets so full that God cannot abide it and pours it out in judgment.

How is it with you? Are you ready? Is everything right between you and everybody? Is everything all right with you? Do you have any habits you should not have? Have you fussed with somebody or lied about somebody or gossiped about somebody and not made it right? Have you forgotten a debt? The statute of limitations has ruled the debt out, and they cannot collect.

Ready
A. C. Palmer (1845–1882)

Ready to suffer grief or pain,
Ready to stand the test;
Ready to stay at home and send
Others if He sees best.

Ready to go, ready to bear,
Ready to watch and pray;
Ready to stand aside and give,
Till He shall clear the way.

Ready to speak, ready to think,
Ready with heart and brain;
Ready to stand where He sees fit,
Ready to bear the strain.

Ready to speak, ready to warn,
Ready o'er souls to yearn;
Ready in life, ready in death,
Ready for His return.

Ready to go, ready to stay,
Ready my place to fill;
Ready for service lowly or great,
Ready to do His will.

17

THE HOLY CITY AND THE BLESSED HOPE

Eternal God and Father of our Lord and Savior, Jesus Christ,
I bow before Thee in expectation of Thy glorious majesty. My hope is not
in this world, but rather in that which You have prepared for me and for
all those who love Thy appearing. Grant me patience while
this world rumbles on in a cycle of monotony. Amen.

The purpose of this book has been to alert Christians to the times in order to prepare for Jesus' return. I have deliberately not focused on dramatic elements of prophecy that seem only to feed the religiously curious; rather my goal has been to feed that blessed hope of the believer. Many become discouraged about prophecy when certain events have not followed what some prophecy teachers taught. For the most part, their focus has been earthbound. However, the old man of God looked for a "city whose builder and maker was God" (Heb. 11:10). Men like Abraham got a glimpse of such a city and lost all interest in things earthly.

It was impossible to move Abraham out of his tent once he got a glimpse of that city. His focus was on that city, and nothing on earth held his interest anymore. After all, how can anything on this earth, tainted by sin, compare with that holy city?

Someone might have gone up to Abraham and asked if he would like to move into a city such as his nephew Lot did. Abraham would smile and get that faraway look in his eye and say, "I'm looking for a city all right. But a city whose builder and maker is God." It is hard for us to explain such a city to those who have never had the vision Abraham had. After all, words could never convey the majesty of such a city. Man at his best has nothing to compare with that city.

God prepared the city John writes about for man. Jesus said, "In my Father's house are many mansions: if it were not so, I would have told you. I go to prepare a place for you. And if I go and prepare a place for you, I will come again, and receive you unto myself; that where I am, there ye may be also" (John 14:2-3). We could, as many have, argue about the word "mansions" and what is actually meant here. Or we could focus on the fact that Jesus has promised to go and prepare a place for us. To define and describe that "place" exhausts the imagination of every man this side of eternity.

The Glory of Man

Perhaps the great hindrance to our envisioning that New City prepared for us is that we have a low view of man. Our picture of man is shrouded in wickedness and depravity. "The heart," Jeremiah the prophet wrote, "is deceitful above all things, and desperately wicked: who can know it?" (Jer. 17:9). All we know concerning humanity are the phrases "deceitful" and "desperately wicked." Although man has fallen, never forget that God created a masterpiece when He created Adam.

One of the supreme glories of man is his many-sidedness. He can be, do and love many things. He is not forced to be one thing, like most other creations. A rock is a rock; a star is a star; a mountain is a mountain. But man is the supreme ruler of cause and effect. He can be a master or a servant; a doer and a thinker; a poet and a philosopher. Man, created by God Almighty, is not a machine made for one operation only. Rather, man is a diamond with many facets to reflect the goodness of the Creator. He can love many things, and if he loves God first, none loses. The key, of course, is putting God first. The sun shines on the whole meadow regardless of what is in that meadow—a mountain, a valley, a river—and no creature is neglected.

The glory of man is also seen in the fact that he is equipped for both solitude and society. Every normal person loves both. "Enter into thy closet" (Matt. 6:6); "Forsake not the assembling of yourselves together" (Heb. 10:25). Every normal person must have time to be alone, to get acquainted with himself and understand his inner thoughts, to aspire and dream and look as far into the future as possible. As Lord George Gordon Byron (1788–1824) wrote:

There is a pleasure in the pathless woods,
There is a rapture on the lonely shore,
There is society, where none intrudes,
By the deep sea, and music in its roar:
I love not man the less, but Nature more,
From these our interviews, in which I steal
From all I may be, or have been before,
To mingle with the Universe, and feel
What I can ne'er express, yet cannot all conceal.

As reaction follows action—the tide, the moon, the day, the season—so man faces those of his kind. This is the reason for all social groups. Whether it is two people keeping each other company in a lonely settler's hut back in the hills, or in a great city where several million people inhabit, people enjoy the company of other people.

The New Humanity

Ideally, we were made for each other. However, sin has entered the picture with greed, hate, power and lust to destroy the glory of that kind of society. It was God's intention in the Garden of Eden that it was not good that man should live alone. And so God brought together Adam and Eve and formed the first society. What a society that must have been without the taint of sin so prevalent today!

I believe that in the final state of perfection, minus sin, the new humanity will dwell in the perfect enjoyment of each other's company. This is what we have in Revelation 21. John calls it the New Jerusalem.

In that blessed society, there will be several aspects we do not enjoy now but which God intended in the very beginning. Everyone will appreciate each other for who they are. No one will be jealous of someone else. No one will look at someone else and covet his or her property and goods. No one will try to subject someone else into servitude labor. No one will suspect of someone else something terrible and take him or her to court.

There will be no slums. How our cities are degraded by this element that seems to be growing with each generation! There is a reason we have slums, and the simple reason is sin. If we could eradicate sin from our society, slums would disappear overnight.

Another quality in this New Jerusalem is that pride will not strut while hunger crawls in these slums. There are so many people today proud of their accomplishments, beating themselves on the chest, getting their names in publications, while across town in the slums, people are starving to death.

Who will dare rise to challenge the desirability of this New Jerusalem? No lover of humanity will. The New Jerusalem will eliminate all the negative aspects of humanity. Throughout history every social dreamer has sought this. Many great men have sought to bring social regeneration to society. Most of them have failed. Each generation seems to be more degenerate than the previous one. Men have worked hard to try to eliminate the negative aspects of humanity, all to no avail; we are worse off than before.

None of it has come through humanity; but John the Revelator saw it descending out of the heavens: "And I John saw the holy city, new Jerusalem, coming down from God out of heaven, prepared as a bride adorned for her husband" (Rev. 21:2).

This is the city seen by men of faith down through the years. Abraham, David, the apostle Paul, the martyrs of the Church—all saw this city John describes here. It is prepared as a bride adorned for her husband. It is the Bride of the Lamb. The city is described as shining in the reflected light of the glory of God.

The All-Satisfying New Jerusalem

The city we look forward to will satisfy man's whole nature. God created man with a certain nature that is compromised, in this life, because of sin. Sin has robbed you and me of this divinely created humanity. But in this New Jerusalem, man's whole nature will be satisfied. It will be a time of celebration as each person realizes the extent and purpose to which he or she was created.

The society in this New Jerusalem will be exactly what God created it to be back in the days of the Garden of Eden. There will be no idleness, for God created man to be a worker. Even Jesus, during His earthly ministry, was known as a worker of good works. There will be no idleness in this New City; but rather man will exercise the full extent of his humanity in doing things reflecting man's glory, which in effect reflects God's glory through the man.

Solitude will be a great pleasure—almost like the old song about heaven, "50 Miles of Elbow Room." Man will be able to explore to the full extent of his nature the delights of solitude and reflection. A man needs plenty of room for reflection these days.

Then, in the New City, there will be permanence. In society today, there is no such thing as permanence. What is in vogue today will very likely be out of focus tomorrow and long forgotten. Nothing in our society is permanent. As soon as you work for and achieve some pleasure, the pleasure is over and the cycle starts all over again. In this New City, there will be a permanence only God can give.

Beauty will be a part of this new city. Nothing ugly will adorn the streets of this New Jerusalem. There will be beauty as coming from the master artist, God Himself. There will be beauty, but not daintiness; a beauty permeates the entire city.

There will be music that will lift the soul Godward. Much of the music we have this side of the New Jerusalem is divisive to say the least. There is no music that enthralls the whole society. Music is broken up into little bits here and there; but in the New Jerusalem, the music will be that which will bless the entire population.

One aspect of the New Jerusalem I particularly am looking forward to is the music. Music has always been an integral aspect of my worship each day. Scarcely a day passes but I open my hymnbook and, slightly off-key, sing one of the great hymns of the Church. My hymnbook is second only to my Bible, and both

I have within easy reach most of the time. There's nothing like a hymn to set my heart in the right direction.

The music of heaven, the New Jerusalem, will be an important aspect of our ecstatic adoration of the one on the throne. In dire contrast, music today serves to divide us in the church. There in that grand city, New Jerusalem, the music will be of such a nature as to bring us into absolute harmony with one another, unknown this side of eternity. Throughout the years, the Church of each generation has been ingenious in the art of the division. Not just theology, but music has been the vehicle of such divisions.

The music in the New City will strike a chord of worship within that cannot be touched today. This music will stir all hearts. It will not be a style of music that defines the worship there, but the Object of worship. Everyone will be on the same tune. The battle about worship and music has so fractured the Body of Christ today that it can only be remedied in the New Jerusalem.

I am anxious for that time. I often get weary of the dichotomy of noise that passes for music in many churches, Bible conferences and camp meetings. In my opinion, the music of the church today can be enjoyed and appreciated by both saint and sinner alike. In the New Jerusalem, only the redeemed will appreciate the musical strains directed toward the throne. Even the angels will stand in silent wonder as the redeemed sing to the Lamb the song of the soul set free.

What an awesome moment that will be when every soul of those redeemed by the Lamb will be free from the carnal accouterments of this world! Free from the "deceitfulness" and "wickedness" that have plagued mankind since the days of Adam and Eve. The sounds will be pure and holy and melodious in the ears of the One sitting on the throne, who alone matters.

Now we usually sing to please ourselves. Then our song will be only to please Him whose ears are altogether pure, holy and righteous. It will be the music of those who have been perfected even as He is perfect. What a choir! There's nothing to compare this side of that New City.

The beauty of that New Jerusalem will be majestic, like the grandeur of the earth. When flying over the Grand Canyon, one can see the breathtaking beauty of nature. Nobody can create beauty like our Creator.

Life in the New Jerusalem will be quite different. Life there will be without sin. Everybody will be safe from the wickedness of the wicked man. No wickedness will walk the streets of that city. Sin will be cast out forever and man will live in the beauty of God's holiness and love. We cannot walk down the streets of any city today without fear of being mugged or robbed. In that new city, no such fear will permeate society. Wickedness will be gone because wicked men will not be there. You cannot define wickedness without pointing to some man. Wickedness is the result of a wicked man; this New Jerusalem will have no wicked men in it whatsoever and therefore wickedness will be a stranger in that city.

Life in the New Jerusalem will be without artificiality. We will be safe from the dullness of mindless man. No longer will we be subjected to boring stories by relatives who have not had a decent thought in decades. In the New City will be men and women whose minds are sharp, whose brains are in full force. Think of the intelligent conversations!

John says, "Behold, the tabernacle of God is with men, and he will dwell with them, and they should be his people, and God himself shall be with them, and be their God." There is no local temple in this city; God Himself is the Temple.

All who enter into the New City are those whose names have been written in the Lamb's book of life. These are men and women who have lived the Blessed Hope all their lives and have brought their lifestyle into absolute harmony with God. The Blessed Hope points us in the direction of that eternal city, the New Jerusalem.

On Jordan's Stormy Banks I Stand
Samuel Stennett (1727–1795)

On Jordan's stormy banks I stand
And cast a wishful eye
To Canaan's fair and happy land,
Where my possessions lie.

O the transporting, rapturous scene
That rises to my sight!
Sweet fields arrayed in living green
And rivers of delight!

There generous fruits that never fail,
On trees immortal grow;
There rocks and hills and brooks and vales
With milk and honey flow.

O'er all those wide extended plains
Shines one eternal day;
There God the Son forever reigns
And scatters night away.

No chilling winds or pois'nous breath
Can reach that healthful shore;
Sickness and sorrow, pain and death
Are felt and feared no more.

When shall I reach that happy place
And be forever blest?
When shall I see my Father's face
And in His bosom rest?

Filled with delight my raptured soul
Would here no longer stay;
Though Jordan's waves around me roll,
Fearless I'd launch away.

I am bound for the promised land,
I am bound for the promised land;
Oh who will come and go with me?
I am bound for the promised land.

18

DAILY LIVE THE BLESSED HOPE

O Christ of the Blessed Hope, how we long for Thee.
The world around us has brought to us a weariness of the flesh.
We are tired of the flesh, the world and the devil, and we
long to come home. This world is not our home, and we are
homesick to come into Thy presence.
Even so, come, Lord Jesus. Amen.

No thesis, no matter how long it is, can give an exhaustive treatment of any subject. Some books claiming to be exhaustive are only exhausting to read. I have not come close to exhausting the subject of the return of Jesus in the book of Revelation. The focus I have tried to keep is that the purpose of prophecy is not merely to alarm us but to alert us to the wonderful truth of the Blessed Hope. Today may be the day He returns, is the believer's anthem.

More things could be said, perhaps even more eloquently than in these pages. But these things are written to alert us to the season of the Blessed Hope. All around us, we have the evidence of Jesus' soon return. Each day our focus should be on the Coming One. Our focus on the Blessed Hope is the most important discipline of our Christian life.

What motivates us determines what we will eventually become. Some are motivated by physical action, while others are motivated by intellectual activity. I believe the only proper motivation for the Christian is seen in this Blessed Hope of which I have been writing. Everything about our daily life must be infused with an insatiable passion for His soon return. As Albert E. Brumley (1905–1977) wrote in "This World Is Not My Home":

This world is not my home, I'm just passing through;
my treasures are laid up somewhere beyond the blue.
The angels beckon me from Heaven's open door,
and I can't feel at home in this world anymore.

A healthy interest in Bible prophecy is not just a casual or curious inquiry. So many Christians are addicted to Bible conferences or workshops where they hear teaching on Bible prophecy. For the most part, these do not change one's life; and although we enjoy the time spent studying the Scriptures on this theme, we leave and go back to life as it was before, unaffected by the truth. The Blessed Hope needs to be infectious in our daily life. It needs to be as essential as the air we breathe.

I began this book on Bible prophecy talking about being cautious and being courageous. We must be cautious not to allow the focus of our study to get off of Jesus Christ. In addition, we must be courageous to keep the central purpose of the Blessed Hope in view and not become stuck in the quagmire of religious trivialities.

Stay Focused on the Heart of Truth

One area where many are careless is in their attitude toward Bible prophecy. There are two sides I would like to emphasize: a dogmatic view versus a charitable view.

Many people have come to the point of being extremely dogmatic about what they believe, and if you do not believe exactly as they do, you are "excommunicated" from their fellowship. Now, there are a few things I am quite dogmatic about and will not back down from for anyone. These are essential core values to Christianity that represent the heart of truth in all generations of Christians. This core of truth is the center of Christianity and defines our fellowship in every generation.

When I was younger, particularly as a young preacher, I had a long list of things I was quite dogmatic about. Many things I refused to move on. Now, as I look back, I am a little bit ashamed of myself. The older I get the less dogmatic I am about certain things.

Certainly, I am dogmatic when it comes to the deity of Jesus Christ, His virgin birth, His blood atonement, His bodily resurrection and the inerrancy of the Scriptures. I could add one more to that list, and that would be the Blessed Hope. I dogmatically believe that Jesus Christ is coming again.

Once I get away from these six areas where I am quite dogmatic, I need to exercise what I call charity. I define my fellowship by these core values; but once I get away from that, do not try to pin me down. Opinions? Yes, I have many opinions. But as I grow older, I have become less dogmatic about my opinions. A person who is dogmatic on many things will come to what I call self-opinionatedness. This person assumes to himself a certain degree of infallibility.

There is a great danger, particularly in the area of Bible prophecy, in being dogmatic about the wrong thing. Let me give you an illustration to explain what I mean here. Let us say, for example, I am in New York City. It is twelve o'clock noon, and I call my friend John who lives in Los Angeles.

"Hello, John. How are things in Los Angeles?"

We talk a little bit, and then I ask John the question.

"John, what time is it there?"

John tells me that it is 9:00 AM. With a very dogmatic attitude, I tell him that he is absolutely wrong.

"I'm looking at my watch right now, John, and it is twelve o'clock noon here in New York City."

"But, Brother Tozer," John says, "I'm in Los Angeles, and it's only 9:00 AM in the morning. I'm looking at my watch right now and it says nine o'clock."

To make matters worse, just when I am dogmatically explaining to John from Los Angeles what time it really is, Brother Tom from London, England, calls me and informs me that it is 5:00 PM in London.

"That can't be," I object. "Brother Tom, I am looking at my watch right now and it says twelve o'clock noon. I'm in New York City, one of the great cities of the world. It cannot be wrong."

I hear Brother Tom chuckling on the other end of the phone, and he says, "Brother Tozer, I'm here in London, England, looking at Big Ben right now, and Big Ben never lies; and it is 5:00 PM."

None of us is right. All three of us are dogmatic about what time it is. We have watches that tell us exactly what time it is. Is it 12:00 noon, as I insist? Or is Brother John on the West Coast right when he says it is 9:00 AM? What about Brother Tom? Does Big Ben ever lie?

This is a rather silly illustration, but it shows just how foolish it is to be dogmatic on some things. This brings me to a very serious question: When will Jesus return? It is very difficult for a dogmatic person to accept the fact that he is both right and wrong. When we come to Bible prophecy, such is the case. Whatever position you take on the return of Christ may differ from where you are standing.

When I am standing in New York City, the time is different from my friend standing in Los Angeles. The time for both of us is different from our friend's in London. To be dogmatic about the time does not advance our fellowship. In fact, we can be so dogmatic about the time that it disrupts our fellowship.

Now we have the 12:00 noon Christians, the 9:00 AM Christians and the 5:00 PM Christians. Who are the real Christians?

Do Not Sacrifice Fellowship for What Doesn't Matter

Could it ever possibly be that all three are right? Is my being right so important that I am willing to sacrifice fellowship over things that are not crucial and central to Christianity?

I have discovered throughout my long career that the best way to evaluate a man is by what he is dogmatic about. If he is dogmatic about everything, that says one thing about him. If, on the other hand, he is dogmatic about the central truths of Christianity and exercises a great deal of charity toward those who have a slightly different view of things, that says something else about that person. I do not mind saying that I want to be among the latter group. I do not want to be so dogmatic about insignificant things that it disrupts fellowship with someone who does not believe all of the elements of Bible prophecy exactly as I do.

What will happen when Jesus returns? Will only those who have the right view go to be with the Lord? Those who had a different view that ended up being the wrong view, would they be left behind? Isn't it silly to be dogmatic about things that the Scripture is not dogmatic about?

When it comes to the fundamental doctrines of the Christian faith, I am as dogmatic as anybody. There are certain truths that I hold on to without apology or without ever backing down. Apart from those central truths, I want to exercise as much charity as possible.

Daily Disciplines for Every Believer

In closing this study, several disciplines need to be in place in our daily Christian life that help us from becoming too dogmatic.

Confess Your Sins

First, I think we must allow no unconfessed sin in our life. Nothing so deteriorates the spiritual atmosphere of our walk with Christ than sin on our shoulders. John Bunyan wrote a whole book, *Pilgrim's Progress,* where Pilgrim carried his sin baggage on his shoulder. Get rid of it. Acknowledge it as sin. Confess it before God and put it under the blood. We must come to a place where we despise sin in every form.

When we come to the life of the believer, we must understand that sin in our life diverts us from that holy expectation of Christ's return. If we believe that Christ is coming today, we would want to deal with all the unconfessed sin in our life. As long as we leave sin unconfessed, we are actually saying that we do not believe the Lord is going to come now.

Sin does many things for the Christian. I think the primary thing sin does for the believer is that it exhausts the believer spiritually. Sin has a way of draining us of the strength we need to live the Christian life, day by day, and it weakens our expectation of the Blessed Hope. Sin also dilutes our spiritual passion and desire until it is so watered down that we have no hope left.

Spend Daily Time in the Word

A daily commitment to the Bible is absolutely essential. I'm not talking about "A verse a day to keep the devil away." I am not sure where that came from, but it certainly did not come from on high. We must so saturate ourselves with the Word of God that our blood becomes, as Charles Spurgeon said, "bibline." I like that.

It is essential that we learn how to read the Scriptures, to meditate upon the Scriptures and discipline ourselves in memorizing Scripture. It is absolutely essential that the Bible have top priority in our thought life. Nothing else should surpass the Scriptures. Everything we do should have roots in the Scripture. Our morning sessions with God over the Scriptures should set forth the pattern and temperament of our daily walk that day. We truly have not read the Bible until we have seen Jesus Christ.

> Break Thou the bread of life,
> Dear Lord, to me,
> As Thou didst break
> The loaves beside the sea;
> Beyond the sacred page
> I seek Thee, Lord,
> My spirit pants for Thee,
> O Living Word.

Perhaps the variety of modern translations mitigate against memorization. But the true believer will rise above this and discover for himself or herself rare treasures to nourish the soul. Here again, let us not be dogmatic about which is the correct translation; rather, let us be dogmatic about reading it with a passion to find Christ and know Him as the Holy Spirit is wont to reveal Him.

Develop an Active Prayer Life

Then there is prayer. It seems so incongruent that everybody believes in prayer and yet few people actually know how to pray, and fewer still practice it with any sort of regularity. Prayer is both the easiest thing to do and the hardest thing we will ever do. There is so much against our prayer life. For one, the enemy of man's soul despises the power of prayer and so, with everything he can muster, he will discourage our prayer life.

I have always appreciated what Dr. Moody Stuart (1809–1898) said in one of his books. He was recording some of the rules that guided him in his prayer life. Let me list them for you right here:

1. "Pray until you pray." I like this one very much. Many people think they are engaging in prayer when what they are really doing is reciting words over and over ad nauseam. Often it takes me 30 to 40 minutes to get into the place where I am actually praying. So many times it is just a mental list, a grocery list, if you please, of what I want God to do for me. Prayer is not something that can be rushed.

2. "Pray until you are conscious of being heard." This, too, is important to grasp. What good is it to pray and pray and then get up off your knees without any sense that God heard you? One of the most important aspects of prayer is penetrating through the "Cloud of Unknowing" and come into the conscious presence of the Lord. This is the objective in all true prayer: to come into the conscious presence of the God whom we serve, love and know with confidence that He heard us. "And if we know that he hears us, whatsoever we ask, we know that we have the petitions that we desired of him" (1 John 5:15).

3. "Pray until you receive an answer." This, too, is rather important. How long should I pray about something? I believe the answer to that is simply that we need to pray until we get the answer. Pray

until we understand what God is trying to do or say in that area of our life. Prayer is not a "hide and seek" game. Prayer is a matter of involving ourselves in a personal relationship, one on one, with God. He delights to open up His heart and show us Himself. He delights to give us that which we are asking.

"If ye then, being evil, know how to give good gifts unto your children, how much more shall your Father which is in heaven give good things to them that ask him?" (Matt. 7:11).

Our prayer life is really the one place in our life where we can practice the presence of the Lord in anticipation of Jesus' soon return. We must penetrate that spiritual obstruction and press on into the presence of our soon coming Lord.

I think we must intentionally cultivate the discipline of seeking the face of God daily. This is something that needs to be a passion of our heart and not merely a routine. As we get on our face before God, we need to do so in the expectation of meeting Him, seeing His face, experiencing the presence—the manifest presence—of this Coming One we are waiting for. It is crucial that we penetrate the veil of the mysterious tremendum. It is not a natural exercise, but rather it is spiritual. Our passion for Christ needs to be carefully nourished with high thoughts about God Himself from the Scriptures.

The whole purpose of these disciplines is to daily wean us from the world. I have often said and will continue to say that the world is too much with us, even in the Church. We must come to the place where the world no longer fascinates us but rather we are highly fascinated with the Blessed Hope. All of these things will create within us an expectation of looking out for the soon return of the Lord Jesus Christ.

Even so, come, Lord Jesus.

Vain Are All Terrestrial Pleasures
David Everard Ford (1797–1875)

Vain are all terrestrial pleasures,
Mixed with dross the purest gold:
Seek we, then, for heavenly treasures,
Treasures never waxing old.

Let our best affections center
On the things around the throne:
There no thief can ever enter;
Moth and rust are there unknown.

Earthly joys no longer please us;
Here would we renounce them all;
Seek our only rest in Jesus,
Him our Lord and Master call.

Faith, our languid spirits cheering,
Points to brighter worlds above;
Bids us look for His appearing;
Bids us triumph in His love.

May our light be always burning,
And our loins be girded round,
Waiting for our Lord's returning,
Longing for the welcome sound.

Thus the Christian life adorning,
Never need we be afraid,
Should He come at night or morning
Early dawn, or evening shade.

EXCERPTS FROM

INSPIRED BY
TOZER

● ●

FEATURING MORE THAN
50 INSPIRATIONAL READINGS FROM WRITERS,
ARTISTS AND LEADERS SUCH AS:
LISA BEVERE, CHUCK SWINDOLL,
KURT WARNER, BEN KASICA (OF SKILLET),
RANDY ALCORN, RAVI ZACHARIAS,
BRITT NICOLE, KENNETH ULMER AND MORE

● ●

LAUREN BARLOW, GENERAL EDITOR

Follow Tozer's new writings on Twitter at
http://twitter.com/tozeraw

GOD
INCOMPREHENSIBLE

CHARLES R. SWINDOLL

AUTHOR, INSIGHT FOR LIVING RADIO HOST AND
SENIOR PASTOR, STONEBRIAR COMMUNITY CHURCH, FRISCO, TEXAS

*Teach us to know that we cannot know, for the things of God knoweth
no man, but the Spirit of God. Let faith support us where reason fails,
and we shall think because we believe, not in order that we may believe.*
A.W. TOZER

Aiden Wilson Tozer died the year I began studying for the ministry. He had spent 31 years pastoring the unobtrusive South-side Alliance Church in Chicago. During his ministry, which included both the spoken and the written word, this intense, provocative man—small in stature but strong of heart—functioned as the conscience of evangelicalism. Yet, I never once heard him speak in person. Nor did most of my contemporary ministerial colleagues.

A. W. Tozer knew God and proclaimed Him fervently. "To listen to Tozer preach was as safe as opening the door of a blast furnace!" said Warren Wiersbe, aptly describing the man's style.

No, I never heard Tozer preach. Yet, in a very real sense, this great man of God lives on, influencing my life and many others, for his pen continues to punch holes in our pseudo-sophistication. It prods us awake when we would otherwise nod off into dreamland.

I haven't counted them recently, but I suppose I have in my possession a dozen or more of Tozer's tough-minded volumes that dare me to drift off course. I don't always agree with him, but he never fails to stimulate my thinking and challenge my walk with Christ. Mystical and severe though he may have been, the man asked the right questions. Questions like: *Is God real to you? Is your Christianity a set of definitions? Is it a list of orthodox doctrines, or is it a vital relationship with Christ? Is your Christianity firsthand and fresh or secondhand? Do you genuinely hunger after God?*

With daring dogmatism, the man didn't stop with casual investigation. He assaulted the status quo with insightful and relentless determination. What he lacked in humor, he made up for in zeal. It didn't take him a hundred pages to get to the point—something most of us would do well to emulate. He pounced like a hen on a June bug—and woe betide the thing within his claws! Those who respect his prophet-like call do not remain the same. *The Pursuit of God, The Divine Conquest, The Root of the Righteous* and *God Tells the Man Who Cares* continue to be some of my most treasured volumes.

With his usual, practical manner, Tozer pinpoints the awe we need to rediscover: "Teach us to know that we cannot know, for the things of God knoweth no man, but the Spirit of God. Let faith support us where reason fails, and we shall think because we believe, not in order that we may believe."[1] The psalmist is correct: The heavens *do* indeed tell of the glory of God . . . their expanse *does* indeed declare the work of His hands (see Ps. 19:1). When you mix that unfathomable fact with the incredible reality that He cares for each one of us right down to the last, tiniest detail, the psalmist is, again, correct: Such knowledge is beyond me . . . I cannot even imagine it (see Ps. 139:6).

Lost in silent solitude, I often have been impressed anew with the vast handiwork of our incomprehensible God. I find His incomprehensibility absolutely refreshing. It is delightful to be reminded that "our God is in the heavens" and that "He does whatever He pleases" (Ps. 115:3, *NASB*). He doesn't ask permission. He doesn't bother to explain. He simply does "whatever He pleases," thank you. After all, He is the Lord . . . the Maker of heaven and earth, the sovereign God of all the universe.

We need that reminder—we who are tempted to think we're capable of calling the shots. How many times must our incomprehensible God tell us that His ways are "past finding out" (Rom. 11:33, *NKJV*) before we begin to believe it? Since the Son of God found it necessary at the crossroads of His earthly existence to pray, "Not as I will, but as You will" (Matt. 26:39, *NKJV*), we would be wise to use the same eight words often . . . every day!

One of the practical ways God's incomprehensibility works itself out is in the pain He allows into our lives. Truth be told, if there is anything that draws us close together as humans, it is this: We all hurt—some more intensely, more deeply or more profoundly than others, but we all know pain. Though we often view it as an enemy, pain is an essential part of God's inexplicable curriculum that leads to obedience.

It's a painful truth: Suffering is essential if we hope to become effective for God. God has at His disposal whatever He wishes to bring into our lives. To the surprise of those who've not stopped to think about it, among those things are suffering and pain. God wants us to be always growing—becoming whole, mature, strong and enduring. He wants us wise and deep, not silly and shallow.

A. W. Tozer was right: "It is doubtful whether God can bless a man greatly until He has hurt him deeply."[2] Solomon, in his journal named Ecclesiastes, wrote:

Consider the work of God, for who is able to straighten what He has bent? In the day of prosperity be happy, but in the day of adversity consider—God has made the one as well as the other (Eccles. 7:13-14, *NASB*).

Psalm 119 echoes this same thought:

Before I was afflicted I went astray, but now I keep Your word. . . . It is good for me that I was afflicted, that I may learn Your statutes. . . . I know, O LORD, that Your judgments are righteous, and that in faithfulness You have afflicted me (vv. 67,71,75, *NKJV*).

If you have reached the place in your Christian life where you are beyond the message of today's superficial theology, you are prepared for this truth. Feel-good, be-happy theology attempts to understand the incomprehensible—to put God in a box. But the pain God allows in our lives breaks the world's mold and renews our minds according to His good pleasure.

Suffering softens our spirits and makes us sensitive to God's voice—for He doesn't leave us alone in our pain. In the stark reality of whatever may be the affliction, God quiets us, calms us and reminds us that everything that occurs reaches us only after being filtered through His hand and permitted for His purposes and glory.

Although this journey along the avenue of affliction is unpleasant and unappealing, it is both inevitable and essential. No one in God's family can remain a stranger to pain and suffering. Working through the hurt is essential if we hope to become effective for God.

The more I ponder the world around us and the universe above us—be it the starry skies, the stormy seas, the majestic mountains or the intense suffering we endure—the more I want to pause, stand still and let the wonder in. Why? Because that's when we see God as who He should be to us—as who He is—namely, *God incomprehensible.* Holy? Of course. Powerful? Yes, no question. Compassionate? Absolutely. Righteous and just? Gracious, loving, self-sufficient and sovereign? All of the above, certainly.

But He is more . . . so much more.

More than we can grasp. More than we can measure or predict. More than the brightest among us can even *imagine.*

What are the benefits of such a realization? We no longer reduce Him to manageable terms. We're no longer tempted to manipulate Him or His Word. We don't have to explain Him and His will or defend Him and His ways. Even when those ways include persistent pain and affliction, we acknowledge His sovereign right to be in full control.

Our God is incomprehensible . . . yet, we long to know more about Him. The words of A. W. Tozer have provided me with a place to begin. How does one embark upon a discovery of who God is?

Humbly. And with awe.

Notes

1. A. W. Tozer, *The Knowledge of the Holy: The Attributes of God: Their Meaning in the Christian Life* (San Francisco: HarperSanFrancisco, 1992), p. 9.
2. A. W. Tozer, *The Root of the Righteous* (Camp Hill, PA: Christian Publications, 1986), p. 137.

If We Would Remember . . .

Bianca Juarez

BIBLE TEACHER, SPEAKER AND FOUNDER,
IN THE NAME OF LOVE MINISTRIES

Oh, if we would only remember who God is!
A. W. TOZER

The edge of the bed was the only stable item in a room that was spinning. I felt short of breath, and the walls of my mind were caving in. On the day I was supposed to be celebrating my twenty-first year of life, I sat on my dorm room bed and felt everything *but* celebratory.

Oh . . .

"Oh," I numbly replied to my father, who waited on the other end of the phone. *Oh* was the only word to fall off my lips. *Oh* was the only word I could say. *Oh* was the only word I felt. My mother was diagnosed with not one, but two forms of cancer on my twenty-first birthday. It was an unnecessary, unwanted birthday gift wrapped in ugly paper.

Oh, if . . .

If it hadn't been finals week, I would've driven to the hospital. If I hadn't been in a dysfunctional, broken relationship, I would've called my boyfriend. If I wasn't feeling anesthetized to life, I would've cried. But I didn't. I sat on a stiff college bed and felt nothing, not even an urge to breathe.

Oh, if we . . .

We had been through so much as a family—but even in financial poverty, God had never let us down. In losses of job, house and car, my father ingrained in us the belief that God would provide. In times of confusion, we were instructed to trust the Lord for direction. In times of plenty, we knew that God was the giver of all, and we owed gratitude to our provider. Now in times of illness I found myself asking, "What if?"

Oh, if we would . . .

Would God take Mom from Daddy? From us? From the church? Would God disappoint the hopes, wishes and prayers from people at our church who *needed* their pastor's wife? Would God forget how she sacrificed for Him, for us, for them? Would God even care?

Oh, if we would only remember . . .

Remembering God's past kindnesses was the last thing on my mind in those first moments after I hung up the phone. Instead, I fell to my knees, and then on my face. Then I curled into a fetal position, overwhelmed by the unanswerable questions. I wept uncontrollably—my tears bitter and my anger at the silence intense. When the anger finally melted, and my cold heart softened, I remembered. I remembered the donated food on our porch when Daddy lost his job. I remembered the car a church friend lent us. I remembered the fact that though my boyfriend didn't love me, God did. I remembered the Red Sea, the manna, the cloud and the pillar of fire. I remembered the fish and loaves, the water and wine, the blind and the sick. I remembered who God said He was.

Oh, if we would only remember who . . .

"Who do you say I am?" Jesus asked this question of His disciples throughout the Gospels, and I had also heard it on the floor of Harris Hall, my college dorm. "Who do you say I am?"

Oh, if we would only remember who God . . .

God—the Alpha and Omega, the beginning and the end, the giver and taker of life. God—the creator of all, the sustainer of all, the lover of all. God—the author, editor and finisher of our faith. God—the first, the last, the eternal. God—caller, listener, speaker. God—healer, rebuilder, restorer. God who loved Adam, loved Esau, loved Judas, loves me. God—almighty, all-powerful, all-knowing. God. God and nothing else.

Oh, if we would only remember who God is!

Heaven's Joy

Dudley Rutherford

SENIOR PASTOR, SHEPHERD OF THE HILLS CHURCH,
PORTER RANCH, CALIFORNIA

*God is going to be as pleased to have you with Him in
heaven as you will be to be there with Him.*
A.W. TOZER

Count me as one of the many who are eagerly awaiting the journey to a place called heaven. What a day that will be when we
get to see our loved ones who have died, exit the struggles and
pains of this life, and experience the place so intriguingly described in Revelation 21:1-27. This vivid passage of Scripture
tells us that the city of heaven will have streets made of pure
gold, walls decorated with every kind of precious stone (such as
sapphires and rubies), and 12 gates made of a single pearl each.
There will be no sun or moon, because heaven will be illuminated by the glory of God. Death and darkness will never enter
this majestic kingdom, and there will be no more sin, sorrow or
sickness. Can you imagine?

Hollywood imagery would lead you to believe that you will
be sitting on a cloud in heaven, strumming a harp all day. But
in actuality, it's going to be a boisterous wedding feast (see Matt.
22:2 and 25:10)—a celebration like no other—and you are going
to *enjoy* yourself! Of course, the ultimate prize is that Jesus will
be there. That's what I'm looking forward to the most. Each of
us, as believers, will be with Christ our Lord for all of eternity,
and we will *never ever* have to say goodbye.

As you look forward to this grand and glorious reunion, it is important to fully absorb what Tozer aptly noted in his surprising statement: God will be just as excited to see you as you will be to see Him—if not more so! But how do we know this?

First, we know it because of the sheer detail that He has put into creating heaven. As a mother bird lovingly and meticulously builds a nest in preparation for the impending arrival of her babies—but in an exponentially greater way—God has been putting the finishing touches on your eternal home. Shortly before His crucifixion, Jesus revealed that He soon would go to His Father's house "to prepare a place for you" (John 14:2, *NKJV*). If the Lord created the splendor of our universe in a mere six days, can you imagine how awesome heaven will be when He has spent the last 2,000 years on its magnificent construction?

Second, we know this because of the depth of God's love. Did you know that He loves you as much as He loves Jesus? That may be shocking, but it's true! According to John 17:23, when praying to God about His earnest desire for unity among all believers, Jesus Himself made this request: "Let the world know that you sent me and have loved them *even as you have loved me*" (*NIV*, emphasis added).

Since God gave up His one and only Son (see John 3:16), it's fair to say He spared no expense in order to get you to heaven. I am reminded of the story of the man who took his son and his son's friend sailing off the Pacific Coast. Though the man was an experienced sailor, he could not foresee a fast-approaching storm that soon pounded their boat with furious waves, causing it to capsize. The three were swept into the ocean. Grabbing a rescue line, the father had to make the most agonizing decision of his life: to which boy he would throw the other end of the lifeline. He had only a few seconds in which to choose. Knowing that his son was a Christian, and that his son's friend was not, the father yelled out, "I love you, son!" and threw the lifeline to his son's friend. By the time the father had pulled the friend back to the capsized boat, his son had disappeared beneath the raging swells.

Romans 5:8 declares, "But God demonstrates his own love for us in this: While we were still sinners, Christ died for us" (*NIV*). God's love for you is unfathomably sacrificial. It can be measured by the dimensions of an old rugged cross at Calvary, upon which Jesus shed His blood for your sins and mine. He loves you, and He wants to spend eternity with you.

When God created Adam and Eve, as chronicled in Genesis 2, He provided everything for them so that they might live in a peaceful paradise and enjoy walking with Him daily. Though they broke that perfect fellowship with their Creator through sin and disobedience, God desired to restore that which was broken and to once again have an intimate and eternal relationship with His children.

Through the death, burial and resurrection of Jesus Christ, our heavenly Father has provided a way for you and me to be reconciled with Him. If you haven't yet put your faith and trust in Jesus, please commit today to follow Him and serve Him. God, like the father of the prodigal son described in Luke 15:11-32, is waiting patiently for you to return to Him—and when you arrive at your heavenly home, He will be so excited to see you. God will announce a celebration of all celebrations, and you will be the object of His eternal joy.

A Tenuous Hope Versus a Certain Truth

Randy Alcorn

Bestselling Author, *Heaven*

The vague and tenuous hope that God is too kind to punish the ungodly has become a deadly opiate for the consciences of millions. It hushes their fears and allows them to practice all pleasant forms of iniquity while death draws every day nearer and the command to repent goes unheeded.

A.W. TOZER

In *The Knowledge of the Holy*, a book that profoundly impacted me when I came to Christ as a teenager, Tozer speaks of the attributes of God, including those we're tempted to minimize. Whether we affirm the holiness and justice of God—and the doctrine of hell, which is inseparable from them—may be the biggest test of whether the Bible or our culture is our true authority.

Without hell, perpetrators of evil throughout the ages would get away with every contemptible deed. But even if we acknowledge hell as a necessary punishment for evildoers, we rarely see ourselves as deserving it. After all, *we* are not Hitler, Stalin or Mao. (Are we?)

God responds, "There is no one righteous, not even one. . . . All have turned away, they have together become worthless; there is no one who does good, not even one" (Rom. 3:10-12, *NIV*).

We consider ourselves good people.

We are dead wrong. To see the face of evil, we need only look in the mirror.

When most people speak of what a terrible notion hell is, they act as if it involves the suffering of innocent people. But nowhere does the Bible suggest that the innocent will spend even a moment in hell!

Tozer wrote, "What comes into our minds when we think about God is the most important thing about us." Many modern Christians have reduced Him to a single-attribute God. Never mind that the angels in God's presence do not cry out, day and night, "Love, love, love," but "Holy, holy, holy is the LORD Almighty" (Isa. 6:3, *NIV*).

By all means, we should rejoice in God's mercy and love. But we must also recognize that our Lord is relentlessly holy, righteous and just. "Your eyes are too pure to look on evil; you cannot tolerate wrong" (Hab. 1:13, *NIV*).

I have spoken at length with a few Christian writers who have reinvented the "good news." They see it not as an offer to be saved from everlasting punishment, but as an assurance that every person, regardless of whether they trust Christ in this life, will spend eternity in heaven. They rob the gospel of its stakes and urgency. They imagine they're paying God a compliment for being so tolerant, but it's not our job to airbrush Him or give Him a facelift.

Ironically, an exclusive emphasis on love strips God's love of its wonder. Without an understanding of the reality and consequences of sin, people aren't surprised by the idea that God loves them—why shouldn't He? But Scripture regards His love for us as remarkable, precisely because of our sin: "God demonstrates His own love toward us, in that while we were still sinners, Christ died for us" (Rom. 5:8, *NKJV*).

When John Newton wrote the hymn "Amazing Grace," he understood what made God's grace amazing—he was a hell-deserving "wretch." When we minimize our sinfulness, we minimize the power and wonder of God's grace. We undermine what God redeemed us for: "in order that in the coming ages he might show the incomparable riches of his grace, expressed in his kindness to us in Christ Jesus" (Eph. 2:7, *NIV*).

What Tozer said 50 years ago could have been written last week:

> A lot of people have talked about the goodness of God and then gotten sentimental about it and said, "God is too good to punish anybody," and so they have ruled out hell. But the man who has an adequate conception of God will not only believe in the love of God, but also in the holiness of God. . . . So let's not write dreamy poetry about the goodness of our heavenly Father who is love— "love is God and God is love and love is all in all and all is God and everything will be OK." That's the summation of a lot of teaching these days. But it's false teaching.[1]

Tozer saw clearly what we need to see. God has already composed His message—it's called the Bible. He doesn't need speechwriters, editors and PR people. He needs faithful messengers.

Though hell is dreadful, it is not evil. Hell is moral, because a good God must punish evil.

Some say, "Maybe hell exists, but surely it's not eternal."

Jesus said, "Then they will go away to eternal punishment, but the righteous to eternal life" (Matt. 25:46, *NIV*). Christ uses the same Greek word for "eternal" (*aionos*) to describe the duration of both heaven and hell.

The increasingly popular doctrine of annihilation merely confirms what most unbelievers already think—that their lives end at death, and therefore no judgment awaits them. We can certainly understand the appeal of such an expectation, but the fact is that Jesus spoke repeatedly of an eternal hell, describing unquenchable fires and the worm that never dies (see Mark 9:48).

In Luke 16:19-31, Jesus taught that an unbridgeable chasm separates hell from paradise. The wicked remain conscious, retain their memories, long for relief, cannot leave their torment, and are offered no hope. Our Savior couldn't have painted a bleaker picture.

Atheist Bertrand Russell wrote, "There is one very serious defect to my mind in Christ's moral character, and that is that He believed in hell. I do not myself feel that any person who is really profoundly humane can believe in everlasting punishment."[2]

Shall we trust Jesus or Bertrand Russell? For me, this is not a difficult choice.

If there isn't an eternal hell, or no one will end up there, Jesus made a huge mistake. If we cannot trust Jesus' teaching about hell, why should we trust anything else He said, including His offer of salvation?

We may pride ourselves in thinking we're too loving to believe in hell. But it's not loving to be silent when people are told the lie that they don't need to turn to Christ in this lifetime to be saved. Are we claiming to be more loving than Jesus, who with outrageous love bore the horrific penalty for our sin?

The Bible speaks of an eternal hell as something that should motivate unbelievers to turn to God, and believers to share the gospel with urgency.

By denying hell, we deny the extent of God's holiness. Worse yet, we deny the magnificence of God's grace. If the

evils He died for aren't big enough to warrant eternal punishment, then perhaps the grace He showed us on the cross isn't big
enough to warrant eternal praise.

The more we believe in *all* of God's attributes, including not
only love and grace but also holiness and justice, the more hell
will make sense to us.

Tozer wrote, "Death fixes the status of the man who loved
his sins and he is sent to the place of the rejected where there is
for him no further hope. That is hell, and it may be well we know
so little about it. What we do know is sufficiently terrifying."[3]

If we are as loving as we claim, we'd better learn to speak
Christ's truth in love—telling people that if they reject the best
gift of a holy and gracious God, purchased with His own blood,
what remains, in the end, will be nothing but hell.

Notes

1. A. W. Tozer and David E. Fessenden, *The Attributes of God, Volume 1: A Journey into the Father's Heart* (Camp Hill, PA: WingSpread, 2003), pp. 107–108.
2. Bertrand Russell, *Why I Am Not a Christian and Other Essays on Religion and Related Subjects*, edited by Paul Edwards (New York: Touchstone, 1967), p. 17.
3. A. W. Tozer, *God Tells the Man Who Cares* (Camp Hill, PA: WingSpread, 1992), p. 39.

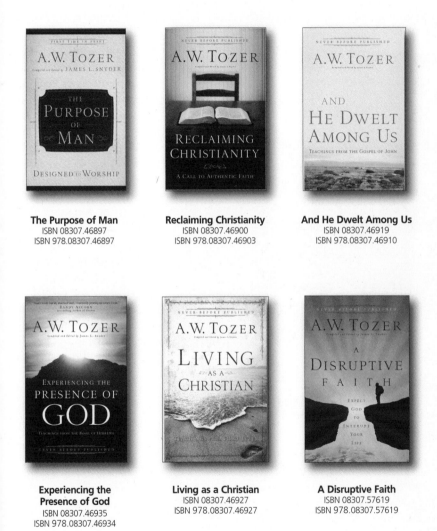

DISCOVER THE CLASSIC WRITER WHO IS STILL CHANGING LIVES TODAY

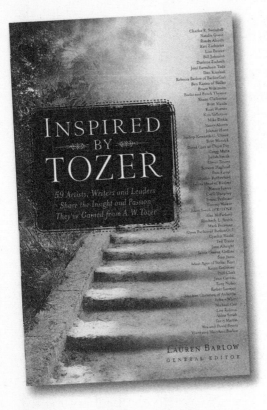

INSPIRED BY TOZER
Lauren Barlow, General Editor
ISBN 978.08307.59293
ISBN 08307.59298

A. W. Tozer lived and wrote a century ago, casting a vision of authentic faith and passionate worship that has taken root in the hearts of each new generation, including young Christ-followers today. In *Inspired by Tozer*, Lauren Barlow, drummer and singer for the award-winning pop group Barlow Girl, has assembled a diverse team of people who, like her, have been inspired by Tozer. Each contributor draws upon a Tozer quote, concept or challenge, and then shares his or her insights, challenging you to move to a deeper place of worship and holy living. These readings will introduce you to one of the Church's most treasured teachers and draw you into a relentless pursuit of God.

INCLUDES ORIGINAL, NEVER BEFORE PUBLISHED WRITINGS BY A. W. TOZER